THE SECRET HISTORY OF THE MONGOLS

The Origin of Chinghis Khan

———————

An Adaptation of the *Yuan Ch'ao Pi Shih*,
Based Primarily on the English Translation
by Francis Woodman Cleaves

By Paul Kahn

NORTH POINT PRESS
San Francisco · 1984

This book is for my grandparents:
Samuel Kahn, Bertha (Kahn) Klein, Herman and Sayde Leben,
and for the Ancestors.

CONTENTS

ACKNOWLEDGMENTS

Many people have helped me in many ways to complete this project, and I would like to take this opportunity to thank some of them. Even before I began work on this book, James Koller's poetry and friendship were an inspiration to me, and it was Jim who first pointed me east from Europe with his own writings about the earliest Central Asian migrations and the Baba Yaga legends. Francis W. Cleaves generously answered my questions about the text in general and his translation of it in particular, and was kind enough to read some of the first sections I completed of my adaptation. Eliot Weinberger gave me valuable criticisms of these first sections and helped me to shake out some of the stiffness in my language. Barbara Norman listened to me endlessly recite passages as I completed them during the first year of the project. Fred and Stephanie Buck and Whitey Morange read a "selected" version of the text and offered me valuable suggestions on how to make some of the difficult passages more understandable. William Corbett, Leslie Scalapino, and Michael Davidson all gave me the opportunity to perform sections of the work at public readings. These were invaluable in getting a sense of what the work sounds like. Albert Craig, as director of the Harvard-Yenching Institute, helped the work into published form. Gary Snyder, whose own work has also been an inspiration to me for many years, gave me the greatest gift of all, his own interest and enthusiasm. Without it this project might never have been completed.

The Text

The text that this book is based on was probably written down in Mongolian during the middle of the thirteenth century, within a few decades of the death of Chingis Khan. The earliest form of written Mongolian made use of a script borrowed from the Uighur Turks. This alphabet was modified to the phonetic requirements of Mongolian so it could be used for recording official documents during the early years of the Empire. It may have been used by this text's anonymous composer during a Great Assembly of the ruling families on the banks of the Keluren River. Internal evidence suggests that the book was to serve as the official account of the origins of the ruling clan of the Mongols, the life history of that clan's late leader, Chingis Khan, and the reign of Chingis's son and successor, Ogodei Khan. The audience for this book would have been limited to the Mongol nobility, perhaps just the royal family itself. Certainly numerous oral traditions would have grown up by this time concerning the monumental feats of Chingis Khan and his contemporaries, and these would have been common knowledge among the camps of the various Mongol clans. This written account appears to be the family's own version of the story, and as such was a form of private property. Several generations later, the Persian historian Rashid al-Din was said to have received much of his information concerning the early years of the Mongol Empire from the Il-khan Ghazan, a Mongol ruler of Persia descended from Chingis Khan, who had learned about it from a "Golden Book" (Altan Debter) which only members of that family were allowed to read. In all probability the present text is a version of this same book.

All of the above is an educated guess, since no manuscript of the original Mongolian version of the text has yet been located. The actual source of the present text is a Chinese manuscript. This book, entitled *Yuan Ch'ao Pi Shih*, (usually translated as *The Secret History of the Mongols*) is traceable to a collection of documents copied out during the Ming Dynasty, after the Mongols had been driven from China. The scribe used Chinese characters to phonetically represent the Mongolian original, and alongside this transcription added a gloss of the meaning in Chinese. The form is much like the interlinear texts prepared by ethnographers from Europe and America when recording oral traditions.

At some point an abridged Chinese translation of the Chinese gloss was added. It was this abridged Chinese translation that was first brought to the West by the Russian orientalist, Palladius, in the late nineteenth century. More complete versions of the Chinese manuscript (including the Chinese transcription of the Mongolian and the Chinese gloss) were published in China during the early years of this century.* Several Old Mongolian manuscripts of similar accounts have been analyzed and translated by scholars since the *Yuan Ch'ao Pi Shih* was first published in Chinese. All this work has only confirmed that the *Yuan Ch'ao Pi Shih* is the oldest version of the story, containing the most complete accounts of the events which led to the formation of the Mongol Empire.

Methodology

Since the Chinese manuscript appeared early in this century it has been translated into Russian, Japanese, German, French, Hungarian, and modern Mongolian. For many years only parts of the work had been published in English translation. Arthur Waley translated sections as prose narrative, based on the abbreviated Chinese translation rather than the full Mongolian, in his *The Secret History of the Mongols and Other Pieces* (1966).† Igor de Rachewiltz has published translations of some sections of the work during the past decade in the Australian academic journal, *Papers on Far Eastern History*, based on the Mongolian original, using both poetry and prose. Paul Pelliot (1949) and Erich Haenisch (1941) both produced translations from the reconstruction of the Old Mongolian, in French and German respectively. As Pelliot died before completing his, Haenisch's German edition was until very recently the only complete version in a European language. These two translations had been the primary published sources of European scholarship on the subject to date. In this tradition of Mongolian scholarship, Francis W. Cleaves translated the entire work into English, with full knowledge of both the Mongolian and Chinese languages, as well as an intimate knowledge of later Mongolian histories. Though its publication was delayed for several decades, copies of the Cleaves translation were circulated and used as a source by various orientalists and historians such as H. Desmond Martin and John A. Boyle as early as the 1940s.

* A detailed evaluation of the various manuscripts and editions that constitute the source of this text can be found in William Hung's "The Transmission of the Book Known as *The Secret History of the Mongols*" in the *Harvard Journal of Asiatic Studies*, (see bibliography at the end of this book) and in Francis W. Cleaves' "Introduction" to his translation of that book.
† A selected bibliography of books in English concerning Mongol history and culture can be found at the end of this book.

Cleaves chose to limit the vocabulary of his translation to the English of the King James Bible in order to convey the archaic flavor of the Old Mongolian language. To make the translation as literal as possible he reproduced the grammatical constructions of the original Mongolian at the expense of common English syntax.

The Cleaves translation was prepared for publication in the 1950s, but its appearance as a book was delayed until its publication by Harvard University Press for the Harvard-Yenching Institute in 1982. I learned about the existence of this translation in 1978 while pursuing independent research concerning the Mongolian Empire. Professor Cleaves generously gave me a copy, and I was able to read the entire text for the first time. I was struck by the many examples of oral poetry that formed the core of the narrative, and the detailed descriptions of the people's lives they contained. I began to rewrite sections of the work using different strategies than Cleaves had chosen. After some initial success, I decided to rewrite the entire work, using the Cleaves translation as my primary guide. The writing of this book has been an act of research and imagination. Having neither travelled in East or Central Asia nor studied the Chinese or Mongolian languages when I began writing, I did not and still do not feel comfortable calling what I have done a translation. Rather I feel this book is an adaptation of the original text as translated by others.

The Chinese manuscript does not indicate any distinction between verse and prose, merely dividing the work into paragraphs which have been consecutively numbered by scholars to identify passages. Translators familiar with Mongolian have rendered many passages as free verse, based on a recognition of the alliterative sequences found in the the original language. Once I had begun I found John R. Krueger's remarks on the nature of Mongolian poetry most instructive.

The major characteristics of Mongolian verse are the presence of alliteration at the beginning of verses, a frequent parallelism of phrasing and internal structure, with a definite tendency to restrict the verses to a fixed number of syllables, usually 7 or 8, but sometimes longer. . . . Mongolian verse does not require (except as some modern authors may choose such forms) a regular alternation of stressed and unstressed syllables according to some predetermined pattern, but it does require alliteration, and without alliteration there can be no poetry in the Mongolian sense of the term.*

I have made every attempt to preserve the parallelism of phrasing and structure, whether the original passage is alliterative or not. This "thought rime" is the

---

* Krueger, *Poetical Passages in the Erdeni-Yin Tobci*, p. 9.

aspect of Mongolian poetry that can best be conveyed in English. An attempt to reproduce the opening alliteration of syllables would be as forced as attempts to translate end rhymes. So far as I know it has wisely been avoided by everyone.

It must be made clear that the original text was not composed as a poem, either in the Euro-Mediterranean or the Mongolian sense of that term as described above. The *Secret History*, being the earliest written document in Mongolian, must have been composed from oral traditions, using various oral organizational techniques. It is a clear example of story-telling as history, a text which records the moment when a culture moved from a system of oral narrative into written history and literature. While it is not correct to say that the original is composed in the form of an epic poem, it is no more correct to say it is composed in discursive prose. I have chosen to adapt the Cleaves translation into the form of a long narrative poem, using an American English vocabulary and grammar. I do not claim to have discovered some previously hidden metric; rather I feel this form is in keeping with the spirit of the original work.

I have replaced the paragraph divisions in the Chinese text, which can occur in the middle of a passage or a sentence, with my own stanza breaks. These new stanza breaks have been made to follow the pauses and shifts of the narrative. Since the convention of using the numbers of the Chinese paragraphs to identify particular passages is already well established in Mongolian scholarship, I have created a table (Table 8) which shows what paragraphs correspond to the text on each page. This is to aid anyone who wishes to compare a particular passage in this book with another translation, or who wishes to locate a passage by its paragraph number.

The *Secret History* is too large to be listened to or read in one sitting, and the twelve "chapter" divisions of the Chinese text seem too arbitrary to warrant reproduction here. To aid the modern reader I have divided the book into five parts. As with the stanza breaks, I have tried to make these divisions reflect the internal structure of the text.

"The Heritage and Youth of Chingis Khan" are described in the first section. Here we are presented with the genealogy of the Mongol clans; a story of their ancestors, Alan the Fair and Bodonchar the Fool; the origin of the conflicts between the Mongol and the Tatar and Merkid tribes; and stories of Temujin's youth from the death of his father to his recapture of Borte from the Merkid. By the end of this part most of the major characters have been introduced, and these early events (the conflicts with Kin, the Tayichigud clan, the Merkid and Tatar tribes, the anda relationships among Temujin, Jamugha, and Toghoril Ong Khan) set the stage for the struggles that follow.

"The Wars In Mongolia" are described in the second part. This section begins with the division of leadership between Temujin and Jamugha, and Temujin's election as Khan of the Mongol clans. The relative strengths of the various clans and tribes wax and wane, with Temujin, now known as Chingis Khan, leading various campaigns against forces that had previously harmed him or now present a challenge to his leadership. Ong Khan and Temujin's father-son relationship is tested, challenged, and finally destroyed, as is the anda-brother relationship with Jamugha. With the absorption of the Tayichigud, Tatar, Kereyid, and Naiman forces, Chingis Khan gains military supremacy over all the major tribes of Mongolia. The section ends with the execution of Jamugha.

"The Developing Empire" begins with the Great Assembly of the Year of the Tiger (1206 A.D.) during which Temujin is once again proclaimed Chingis Khan, now ruler of all the tribes of Central Asia. A great deal of this section is devoted to accounts of the rewards given to Temujin's supporters by the new supreme Khan, and a description of the military organization of the allied tribes. This section recounts several later conflicts including the challenge to Chingis Khan by the shaman Teb Tengri.

"The Wars in Cathay and the West" contains the Mongolian account of the military campaign in northern China and the Middle East. This begins with a campaign against the Kin Dynasty during the Year of the Sheep (1211). The wars against the Kin and the Tanghut are described, followed by an account of the choosing of Ogodei as Chingis Khan's successor. This is followed by an account of the Middle Eastern wars and mention of the first expedition into southern Russia. The section ends with the death of Chingis Khan during the final campaign against the Tanghut in 1227.

"The Reign of Ogodei Khan" begins with his election during the Great Assembly in the Year of the Rat (1228/9). The war against the Kin is completed, woven into an account of Tolui's death. Brief mention is made of the renewed campaigns in the Middle East and Eastern Europe. Several of the members of the next generation who play prominent roles in the history of the Mongolian Empire are mentioned, including Guyuk, Mongke, Buri, and Batu. The section ends with a brief summary of the accomplishments and faults of Ogodei Khan and a colophon identifying where and when the text was recorded.

I have also added "The Origin of Chingis Khan" to the usual English title. This is from the first line of the Mongolian text, which has been translated as "the origin(s) of Chinggis Qahan." It seems likely that this first line may be the Mongolian title of the text. "Yuan ch'ao pi shih," clearly of Chinese origin,

xv

means literally "the Yuan (i.e. Mongol) Dynasty's private history" and is usually translated as "The Secret History of the Mongols." So I have simply taken this first line of the Mongolian text and moved it from the text into the title.

The accuracy of my version is dependent on my interpretation of the primary scholarship of Cleaves and several other sources. In particular, it is Professor Cleaves who has rigorously cross-referenced the text, noting the many repetitions of phrasings, descriptive formulas or metaphors, and in some cases entire passages. I have tried to maintain this structure of repetition, so that my choice of phrasing in one passage is consistent with the same phrasing when it occurs later in another passage. I have also had the advantage of John A. Boyle's beautifully annotated translations of Juvaini and Rashid al-Din's Persian histories and have benefited a great deal from translations of Rene Grousset's many books on Central Asian history. While I have had the advantage of taking what I can from these superb guides, I alone am responsible for the choice of form and vocabulary, and for the interpretation of passages where current scholarship has been unable to clarify an ambiguity in the text.

In transcribing Mongolian names I have followed a few principles which should be explained. There is no standard method of transcribing Mongolian, and I have chosen to use what I judged to be the most common version of a name or the one easiest to pronounce in English. I have used "kh" for "q" (khan rather than qan), and have avoided diacritics or non-English letters used by some Mongolists by simply substituting less exact English consonant combinations such as "ch," "gh," and "sh." Where some transcriptions of Mongolian names use the single apostrophe to indicate a glottal stop, I have uniformly substituted the consonant "g" so that Ho'elun becomes Hogelun and Tayichi'ud becomes Tayichigud. This hard "g" sound appears to be close to modern pronunciation. Most Mongolian names in the text consist of two words, the first being a proper name and the second an epithet or clan identification. I have translated some of the common epithets when the literal meaning of the name seemed appropriate. Bagatur is translated as the Brave, Boko as the Athlete, Sechen as the Wise, Mergen as the Clever, Kulug as the Hero, and Ghoa as the Fair. Following this system, Yesugei Bagatur is rendered as Yesugei the Brave, and Dei Sechen becomes Dei the Wise. Mongolian titles, such as Khan, Khatun, Ujin, and Beki, are left untranslated, since their European equivalents (king, queen, lady, chieftain/priest) would be misleading. The meaning of these titles becomes evident in the context in which they are used.

This book is an adaptation of the entire *Secret History*, with some selective omissions. Among these are sections of the early genealogy that list the names of each generation of ancestors, and passages explaining the etymology of some clan names. I have edited out proper, clan, or geographical names throughout where such additional detail served more to confuse than to clarify the narrative. Several short passages dealing with characters who do not otherwise appear in the story have been omitted for the same reason. The only large section omitted is a repetition by Ogodei Khan of the elaborate assignment of the royal guard. The purpose of this passage is to name the men serving the new Khan in a manner parallel to the naming of the men who had served Chingis Khan in an earlier passage. As it comes at the end of the book and none of the men named play any further role in the story, I have left the entire section out for the sake of economy. Where necessary, I have added information which the composer omitted, perhaps because the thirteenth-century listener would have found that information superfluous. I have tried to make the story understandable to a contemporary audience with no special training in the culture of medieval Central Asia and have chosen to add necessary information directly in the text rather than resorting to footnotes.

Twelfth-Century Asia

The events described in the *Secret History* take place in the geographical area now within the borders of the Soviet Union, Mongolian People's Republic, People's Republic of China, Afghanistan, and Pakistan. In the West, Islamic culture stretched from the Iranian plateau toward the northern frontier of Chinese culture via the string of oasis cities along the Tarim Basin to the Hindu Kush. These islands of agriculture and urban civilization were politically represented by a series of small kingdoms and city-states. The entire area now falls within the borders of Soviet Central Asia on the Russian side and Sinkiang (Xinjiang)* Province in China. The Chinese state had controlled the entire region up to the Hindu Kush during the Tang Dynasty two centuries before, but by the 1100s the Chinese had dropped active contact and trade relations with the West. This was because China itself was fragmented into three kingdoms.

Since the fall of the Tang Dynasty northern China had been ruled by non-Chinese people. The first of these rulers were the Khitai (Ch'i-tan), a Central Asian tribe native to the Mongolia-China borderlands. The Khitai were one of a series of steppe or northern forest peoples who have ruled this part of China periodically, when Chinese political organization has been in decline. The name Khitai became the Mongol and Russian word for China itself, and via the writings of Marco Polo, became "Cathay" in European literature.

---

* I have placed variant spellings of Chinese words in parentheses.

In 1125 the Khitai themselves were overthrown and succeeded by a tribe from the Manchurian region, known as the Jurchid. Both tribes took on Chinese political forms, including dynastic titles; the Khitai had ruled as the Liao Dynasty, taking the name of a river in their native region, and the Jurchid chose the title Kin (Chin or Jin), meaning "gold." In a mixture of ethnic titles and languages typical of Central Asian culture, the twelfth-century Mongols referred to this Jurchid ruler as the Golden King (Altan Khan) of the northern Chinese kingdom they still called Cathay (Khitad). To be consistent with this Mongol usage, I have chosen to use the name Cathay to refer to the northern Chinese kingdom in the present text. When the Khitai were overthrown by the Jurchid, a part of their ruling family fled with an army west onto the steppe near Lake Balkhash, where they established a new kingdom. This kingdom is referred to as Black Cathay (Khara Khitai) in the Mongol text.

The Chinese ruling class had fallen back to the south of the Yellow River (Huang-ho), much as they had centuries before after the disintegration of the Han state. Here they ruled as the Sung (Song) Dynasty, claiming to be the preservers of true Chinese culture. On their western border, in what is now Kansu (Gansu) Province and eastern Tibet, was another autonomous kingdom, ruled by a Tibetan people, who called themselves the Minyag. These people were called the Tanghut by the Mongols, and their capital city was Ning-hsia (Ning-xia) on the upper reaches of the Yellow River. The Chinese called their kingdom the Hsi Hsia (Xixia) or Western Kingdom.

The northern border of the Kin and Tanghut kingdoms was the Great Wall and the Gobi Desert. Beyond this lived various tribes of mixed ethnic background, who nomadized on the steppes which extended from the arid Gobi in the south to the shores of Lake Baikal and the Siberian forest in the north, and stretched westward into southern Russia. The names of major tribes who figure in the present narrative are the Tatar, Mongol, Merkid, Naiman, Kereyid, and Oyirad.

The *Secret History* begins in the time when the first ancestors of the Mongol tribe came across the "inland sea" (called Tenggris in the text, probably meaning Lake Baikal) to settle near the source of the Onan River in what is now western Mongolia. The lineage begins with the animal pair of a wolf and deer, and then proceeds through several generations to members of indigenous tribes which appear again later in the story, such as Uriangkhai and Tuman. What is interesting about tracing this lineage of ancestors, beginning with the son of the wolf and deer and pausing at the five sons of Alan the Fair, is how it does not follow any stable pattern of transmission. Strength alone determines who becomes the leader in the next generation. The hero of this ancestor myth, Bodonchar the Fool, is the youngest son of an unidentified father (Table 1). His greatest talent is his ability to use the predatory strength of others (a falcon, wolves, his four brothers) to his own, and ultimately his family's, advantage. He is referred to later in the text as "Holy Ancestor Bodonchar" and several important clans traced their lineage from his issue. The primary lineage is that of the Borjigin clan, into which Temujin (the future Chingis Khan) was born.

The political situation that preceded Temujin's birth was centered on conflict between the Mongol and Tatar tribes. The Mongol had been organized under a central leader for several generations. This leadership role was passed in the mid 1100s to Ambaghai Khan, the senior patriarch of the Tayichigud clan (Table 2). The Kin, as part of a long Chinese tradition of using one "barbarian" people to weaken another, encouraged conflict between the Tatar and Mongol. The *Secret History* is sketchy about why the Tatar captured the Mongol leader; Grousset adds several details which were perhaps common knowledge to a Mongol audience. Ambaghai had arranged a marriage alliance with one of the ruling families of a Tatar clan. Acting as an instrument of Kin policy, another Tatar clan took him as a captive and turned him over to the Kin, presumably for some substantial reward. The Kin then had Ambaghai executed. It is interesting to note how the same situation appears in reverse later in the story. The Tatar had become too strong in the eyes of the Kin, and now it is the young Temujin and his Kereyid allies who are used to attack a Tatar camp that is fleeing from an advancing Kin army. These "barbarian" leaders are then rewarded by the Kin general for their service with Chinese titles. The repercussions of Ambaghai's betrayal by the Tatar and execution by the Kin were to echo for many generations, as the Mongol tribes first became committed to a war of revenge against the Tatar, and then a war of domination against the Kin. That war in turn expanded until the Sung were also conquered, and all of China was ruled by the Mongols under the Yuan Dynasty.

At the time of Temujin's birth there was no central power in Mongolia. The war of revenge between the Mongol and the Tatar was being waged indecisively. Temujin's father, Yesugei the Brave, was a direct descendant of Khabul Khan, who had ruled the Mongol before Ambaghai (Table 3). He had evidently proven himself to be a strong leader during this war. As a result Yesugei had become the leader of a large camp, consisting of families from his own Borjigin clan as well as members of Ambaghai's clan, the Tayichigud.

Mongol Culture before the Empire

The Family. One of the central facts of the *Secret History* is the family unit. The ancestry myth of Alan the Fair and her five sons is a parable of how this unit can interact in either a self-destructive or cooperative manner. The social context the family operates in is the camp rather than the village or city. That context provides a double-edged freedom. To survive on the steppe a sophisticated nomadic culture had developed over the past two milleniums, based on herding of horses, sheep, camels, oxen, and goats. Everything was mobile, and as a result families could move not only from region to region as climate and season required, but also from camp to camp, as the fortunes of a clan would wax and wane. A charismatic or fortunate leader would attract a large camp in a short period of time. Conversely, when a leader died or times got bad due to disease, bad weather, or war, a camp could easily break up. The manner in which a family's wealth was divided among the male children could also easily lead to a family's dissolution, as each new sub-family moved away to fend for themselves.

In the story of Chingis Khan's youth, we have numerous examples of how his mother, Hogelun, fought to keep her small family alive and united after they had been expelled from the camp her late husband had gathered. Her sons (Table 4) display the full spectrum of possible intrafamily behavior, from fratricide (when Khasar and Temujin kill Begter) to complete support at the risk of great personal loss (when Khasar leaves his own family with the Kereyid to join Temujin's forces at Baljun). Certainly one strong moral theme in the *Secret History* is the importance of cooperation and mutual respect within the family unit. Whenever Chingis Khan forgets these principles, his mother or one of his wives does not hesitate to step forward and correct him with an impassioned speech. In fact all the major speeches concerning family loyalty are delivered by or about women.

The account of how Chingis Khan chooses his third son, Ogodei, to succeed him also illustrates the importance placed on maintaining family harmony in the face of obvious tensions. In choosing Ogodei as the next Great Khan, Chingis is clearly trying to respect the family tradition of dividing the territory among his sons, while establishing a mediating figure that the entire family would respect. The traditional way in which a family's wealth was divided was to give the eldest son the territory farthest from the original home pasturage. The home pasturage and the father's own possessions were left to the widow and the youngest son, known as the Odchigin, a name sometimes translated as "prince of the hearth" or "fire prince," i.e., ruler of the home fire. This is the role that falls to both Chingis Khan's youngest brother, Temuge Odchigin, and later to his youngest son, Tolui. When Chingis Khan divides the people after his second coronation in 1206, we see him giving the largest portion jointly to Hogelun and Odchigin, and Odchigin is left to rule the Great Camp when his older brothers go off to war. Tolui also inherits the home territory, which by the time of his manhood has come to mean all of Mongolia. Chingis Khan's eldest son, Jochi, is given the territory farthest from home to rule. This was southern Russia, and it was Jochi's eldest son, Batu, who established himself at Sarai on the Volga during the middle thirteenth century as the ruler of the Golden Horde. In keeping with the same family tradition, we see Ogodei Khan issue a decree calling on everyone to send their eldest sons off to aid in the war against Kiev. This is the only reference in the *Secret History* to the army which invaded Eastern Europe in 1240, as the eldest sons of the united tribes of Central Asia fought their way across Russia, Hungary, and Poland.

Marriage. The various tribes in Mongolia appear to have all practiced some form of exogamy; a man had to find a wife someplace other than his own clan or tribe. This must have been a major source of inter-tribal contact. In some circumstances marriages were arranged by parents, gifts were exchanged, and feasts and other ceremonies gave clans and tribes an opportunity to mix in a peaceful manner. The woman entered another clan to establish her family, and each family was a mixture of clan or tribal blood and traditions. In other circumstances marriages were the result of raids, abductions, or warfare. This is how Yesugei comes to marry Hogelun; he sees her riding by, chases off her Merkid husband, and takes her back to his own camp. Marriage by abduction was just cause for revenge on the part of the tribe who had lost their women without proper payment or ceremony. All the battles between Chingis Khan and the three Merkid clan chiefs in this story are said to be caused by this initial act of wife-stealing.

All the tribes also practiced polygamy. Having more than one wife was a sign of wealth and political power. The first wife held certain unique privileges, the most important of which was that the succession went to her sons. She also could inherit the power of her husband if one of her sons was not an obvious successor. We see Hogelun attempt to seize her late husband's leadership role, when she is being driven away by the leaders of a rival clan. While Borte, Chingis Khan's first wife, did not have to serve in this capacity when her husband died since the roles her sons would inherit had all been made clear, Ogodei's wife, Doregene (also spelled Toragana in some sources), served as regent of the Empire for five years, from the time her husband died until her son, Guyug, was elected to succeed him. Tolui's wife, Sorkhaghtani, also served as regent between the reign of Guyug and that of her own son, Mongke Khan. Chingis Khan took many wives (Table 5), and in his case marriages, whether the result of warfare or diplomacy, were a means of interweaving the various royal families of Central Asia with his own.

Class Structure. The population of the Mongol and other tribes was also divided into social classes. The *Secret History* is primarily the story of the noble class, that is those people directly descended from the leaders of the previous generation. Members of the nobility expected a certain support from the rest of the population, who acted as their retainers, their herdsmen, their soldiers, etc., and in a sense agreed to be ruled by a particular noble or clan chief. This common class contained people of various levels of wealth, and their personal freedom was dependent on the strength or style of the leaders they served. The loyalty a leader could instill in his followers was of primary importance. A major theme in the *Secret History* is that loyalty to a rightful leader is always to be rewarded, and treachery to be punished. Chingis Khan refers to this at one point as "the great principle" and in this world of quickly shifting fortunes we can easily see why.

Below both the noble and common class was a class of slaves or servants, made up primarily of war captives. Warfare between two tribes would often result in the capture and absorption of one population into another. The men of fighting age would be killed or given menial positions such as goat or camel herders and the rest of the defeated population would be distributed among the victors' households as personal servants. In this way members of the noble class could become slaves if their clan was defeated in war.

Conversely, servants or commoners could raise their status by serving a strong member of the noble class as personal retainers. As their loyalty was rewarded their own wealth and status would grow. This is the context in which we see commoners such as Jelme "given" to Temujin when both men are still infants, and others such as Mukhali offered to Chingis Khan as personal slaves by their families. This is also the context in which former enemy soldiers such as Jebe offer their services to the leader they had been fighting moments before. Once a man had fulfilled his obligation to defend his leader, and that leader was defeated, the man was free to offer his services to the victor without being guilty of disloyalty.

Religion. While there is a good deal of religious ceremony and reference in the *Secret History* there is little said about religion itself. Traditional Mongol religion is usually described as a form of shamanism, and consists of a belief in various gods (tengri). The most prominent of these in the *Secret History* is Eternal Blue Heaven (Koko Mongke Tengri). It is Eternal Heaven that appears to be guiding Chingis Khan throughout the story, and all of his successes are attributed by him to Heaven's will. In addition there is a special ceremony observed to the mountain Burkhan Khaldun for its protection of the hero and his family, which suggests that the spirit of the mountain was also treated as a god. The practice of burying particularly important men on mountains or prominent cliffs is also found in the story, and may have been related to mountain worship. The number three seems to have been sacred, as was nine (three threes), and both numbers are used in many descriptive formulas throughout the story. Several characters are described as performing shamanistic feats, such as raising a storm of darkness (jada) or conversing with spirits. We see how in the case of Teb Tengri and Toghtoga Beki, shamanic and political powers were closely related. Beyond that little is said explicitly about the religious beliefs and practices of the people. How the Mongol priesthood worked, if it existed in any formal way at all, remains a mystery.

At the same time forms of Christianity and Buddhism were present in Mongolia, and Islam and Taoism were present on its borders. The Kereyid and Onghut tribes both contained many Nestorian Christians. The Tanghut were a Tibetan Buddhist people, and the Uighur practiced a Turkish form of Buddhism which has since disappeared. To the Mongol this all seems to have been unimportant. There is no mention of Christianity in the *Secret History* though a few Christian Kereyid and Onghut names occur in the text. The only reference to Buddhism is the mention of golden images offered by the Tanghut ruler as tribute to Chingis Khan. The Mongol nobility was tolerant of all forms of religion, but did not become interested in Buddhism and Islam as personal faiths for several generations.

There is certainly no identification by the Kereyid characters with the Christian West, though the converse was probably true. As Grousset and others have pointed out, the medieval European legend of Prester John, the great oriental warrior-king, may have been based on garbled accounts of the Kereyid leader, Toghoril Khan, and his "son" Chingis Khan.

Temujin's Rise to Power

The bulk of the *Secret History* is a uniquely detailed account of how the eldest son of a nobleman from the Borjigin clan, born sometime in the 1160s, rose to be first the ruler of the united Mongol clans, then the conqueror of all the nomad tribes, and finally the "world conqueror" as the Persian historian Juvaini called him, who successfully waged wars against the agricultural and urban cultures of China and the Middle East. This remarkable man was first given the name Temujin, after a Tatar warrior his father captured shortly before his birth.

Before Temujin was born, his father Yesugei had also made an alliance with the leader of the Kereyid tribe, Toghoril Khan. This alliance was in the form of an "anda" bonde a custom which figures prominently in the story. The pledg of an anda relationship between two men was a special acknowledgment by both parties that they had agreed to aid each other under any circumstances. In the case of Yesugei and Toghoril it was made in appreciation for special aid of-fered by Yesugei to the Kereyid leader in a time of distress. Toghoril had per-secuted his own brothers in order to consolidate his leadership position, and had been driven into exile by an army led by his uncle. At Toghoril's request, Ye-sugei raised an army from the Mongol clans and restored the Kereyid leader to his throne. The anda pledge which Toghoril offered as a kind of spiritual re-payment carried with it responsibilities analogous to family bonds. Because of this anda pledge, Yesugei and Toghoril were "brothers" and also had the role of "father" to the other man's children.

A second anda bond was made by Temujin himself, with a nobleman his own age from the Jadarin clan, known as Jamugha. This bond was first made in childhood, and then renewed when the two men were young chieftains. The spiritual authority these extra-familial bonds carried, and the tensions that re-vulted from them, are a major factor in the story of Temujin's early life. In order to understand many of his actions, and the elaborate justifications he gives for each, we must remember the sacred nature of these anda bonds, and observe how carefully Temujin employs them. He and Jamugha repeatedly refuse to do each other direct harm, though they are bitter rivals during much of the story. Toghoril himself is faced with the dilemma of choosing between support for his adopted son, Temujin, or his natural son, Senggum. It is clear that he inter-prets this as an unhappy choice between sacred and familial obligations, and that by choosing to go with his own family he has seriously offended the gods. The psychological dimension of these anda bonds also gives the story of Te-mujin's youth an element of classical drama. Having lost his own father at the age of nine, we see him first saved and then betrayed by his spiritual father and brother. We then see him struggle to overcome the treachery of this spiritual family, always carefully staying in the grace of Heaven, in order to realize his own destiny as founder of a nation.

Temujin was later given the name Chingis Khan, a name by which he is known throughout the world. The name is sometimes spelled Genghiz, Jenghiz, or Tchingis. In the *Secret History* he receives this name when he is elected khan of the Mongol by his uncles and cousins, the various clan leaders. This first coronation took place during the last decade of the twelfth century. It involved an oath of allegiance from the Mongol clan leaders, and the organization of a personal army. This bodyguard was under the direction of Temujin's early retainers, men such as Bogorchu and Subetei, who were later to become his great generals. The years that followed are described in great detail in this story, and by the end of the century Chingis Khan had built a single nation out of a diverse population. In 1206,* a date corroborated in the *Secret History* and other sources, a second coronation was held and Chingis Khan was recognized as supreme ruler of the new nation he had forged. This second coronation is described in the text as an elaborate occasion at which the Great Khan rewarded all the men who had served him up to this point by assigning them subjects to rule and other social privileges.

The word "chingis" is not translatable. Juvaini suggests that it may have been given to Temujin by the shaman Teb Tengri, and as such may have had an esoteric shamanic meaning which has been lost. It is usually said to be related to the term "oceanic" meaning all-powerful and all-encompassing. In this sense the name was a fitting description of what Temujin had accomplished by consolidating his power over all the tribes in Mongolia. Following the second coronation, we see how the various rulers of other Central Asian kingdoms fell in line and recognized the new Chingis Khan as their ruler, cognizant perhaps of the old Turkish Empire which had unified the steppe region centuries before. Once all the people of Central Asia recognized his power, the Mongol ruler turned his newly swollen armies toward the wealthiest culture of his day, the urban centers of China.

The wars against the Kin and Tanghut kingdoms in China are left rather sketchy in the *Secret History*, as is the later war against the Khwarezm kingdom, which was located in parts of present-day Soviet Central Asia, Afghanistan, Iraq, and Iran. The only details of these wars that were important to the Mongol chronicler were which commanders or princes were responsible for which victories, and what conflicts arose among the Mongols themselves. The sequence of how the actual campaigns were fought are either wrong or greatly abbreviated. During the first war against China the Mongol army attacked the Tanghut first, and then used the Kansu (Gansu) corridor to attack the Kin from the west rather than the north where they were expected, fighting their way to the plains surrounding the Kin capital at Chung-tu, near present-day Peking (Bei-

---

* Dates in the text are given by moon and animal year, according to the Chinese system also used by the Mongol. A chart of the animal year cycle and the corresponding years in the Christian calendar is found in Table 7 at the end of the book.

jing). The *Secret History* would lead us to believe that the Kin were attacked first via the pass at Chu-yang Kuan (Juyongguan), the Chu-yung Kuan of the text, just north of their capital, and that the Tanghut were dealt with later. The war against the Arabo-Persian culture of Khwarezm was a long and complex campaign, lasting over six years. The provocation that started the war, alluded to in the *Secret History* as the killing of "the hundred ambassadors led by Ukhuna," is described in greater detail by Juvaini. The Mongol court, enriched by the spoils of victory against the Kin and Tanghut, had sent a trade caravan led by the envoy Ukhuna to the Khwarezm court, to begin an exchange of treasures such as precious metals for Persian luxuries such as fine cloth. Juvaini's account, written down a generation after the event took place, offers these details:

When the party arrived at Otrar, the governor of that town was one Inalchukh, who was a kinsman of the Sultan's mother, Terken Khatun, and had received the title of Ghayir Khan. Now amongst the merchants was an Indian who had been acquainted with the governor in former times. He now addressed the latter simply as Inalchukh; and being rendered proud by reason of the power and might of his own Khan [Chingis Khan] he did not stand aloof from him nor have regard to his own interests. On account of this Ghayir Khan became annoyed and embarrassed; at the same time he conceived a desire for their property. He therefore placed them under arrest, and sent a messenger to the Sultan in Iraq to inform him about them. Without pausing to think the Sultan sanctioned the shedding of their blood and deemed the seizure of their goods to be lawful, not knowing that his own life would become unlawful, nay a crime, and that the bird of his prosperity would be lopped of feather and wing. .... Ghayir Khan in executing his command deprived these men of their lives and possessions, nay rather he desolated and laid waste a whole world and rendered a whole creation without home, property or leaders. For every drop of their blood there flowed a whole Oxus; in retribution for every hair on their heads it seemed that a hundred thousand heads rolled in the dust at every crossroad; and in exchange for every dinar a thousand khintars of gold were exacted.*

The Khwarezm Shah, known as Sultan Mohammud, was not able to muster effective resistance to the Mongol invasion. It was his son, Jalal al-Din, who led the only serious challenge the Mongols faced, and it is his name that is recorded in the *Secret History* as the leader of the Moslem forces. The order of the campaign is greatly abbreviated. The battle on the banks of the Indus during which Jalal al-Din escaped by swimming the river and fleeing into India took place late in the war, rather than at its beginning. The massacre of entire urban pop-

* From *The History of the World Conqueror* by Juvaini, J. A. Boyle translation, Volume I, pp. 79–80.

ulations and the destruction of ancient cities by the Mongol armies is simply not mentioned. We get no hint of how the techniques of Mongol warfare had developed during the wars in China. Jurchid and Khitan engineers were employed to operate siege engines against the cities of Khwarezm, and captured populations were pushed before the advancing armies as a kind of pre-artillery cannon fodder. The delicate balance that had existed for centuries between the nomadic and urban civilizations in western Asia was suddenly destroyed, and the Moslem intelligentsia found themselves in the service of the nomad ruling house. For decades it seemed as though nothing on the face of the earth could stop the Mongol cavalry, except the tropical heat of India.

The second Tanghut war is depicted in the *Secret History* as a campaign of retribution. The Tanghut ruling house had refused to support the Mongols during the invasion of Khwarezm with troops, and Chingis Khan is shown as determined to repay that insult with a massive show of force. Luc Kwanten cites other sources that suggest the Tanghut may have struck an alliance with the surviving Kin forces, in an attempt to drive the Mongols from China.* Unlike the kingdom of the Khwarezm Shah, the Tanghut culture left no chronicle of its own destruction, and so we may never know the details of how it came to an end. Chingis Khan died during the campaign, having lived into his sixties, and was returned for secret burial in Mongolia during the summer of 1227. Later Mongolian histories, such as the *Erdeni-Yin Tobci* dating from 1662, include beautiful elegies for him, picturing him as a great culture hero with supernatural powers. A cult honoring his remains survived into the present century in the Ordos region of China. The *Secret History* simply mentions Chingis Khan's death in passing, as an "ascension," and does not dwell on any funeral details. The emphasis is on the orderly transition of power within the royal family. Battles were still being fought in China and the Middle East when Chingis died. Subetei had returned from his first raid around the Caspian Sea into southern Russia. In two decades the Mongol armies had ridden across most of Eurasia and never suffered a serious defeat. Unimagined wealth was pouring into Mongolia. What had begun as new territory captured in raids was quickly becoming the largest empire ever created.

Ogodei's Reign

Control of the new empire went to Chingis Khan's third son, Ogodei. Ogodei had been chosen by his father, and this choice was confirmed by the surviving

---

* Kwanten, *Imperial Nomads*, p. 92.

elders of the royal family in 1229 at a Great Assembly in Mongolia. The three-fold military strategy of the new Great Khan is recorded in the last sections of the *Secret History*: a renewed war of conquest to finally annihilate the Kin forces in Northern China; reinforcing the Mongol army in the Middle East; and conquest of the steppe region of Russia and Eastern Europe. In addition to these military moves, Ogodei was also responsible for consolidating the administrative structure of the Empire. The new Mongol capital at Kharakhorum (Black Rock) was built, a city later described by the European missionaries John of Plano Carpini and William of Rubruck. A mixture of Persian, Khitan, Jurchin, and Chinese officials was integrated into the Mongol government as important ministers, and with them came the administrative traditions of China and Persia. An elaborate postal system was set up to carry messages from one end of the vast Eurasian landmass to the other.

The only war Ogodei took part in himself was the campaign in China early in his reign. He suffered an apparent stroke during the fighting, perhaps already suffering from the alcoholism that was to kill him. The account of this in the *Secret History* is woven into the story of Tolui's death. The internal politics of this text are clearest in this story and the later story of Ogodei's punishment of his son, Guyug, for insubordination during the Russian campaign. Though Juvaini records that Tolui died of too much alcohol after returning victorious from the campaign in China, here his death is an heroic sacrifice for his elder brother. Tolui and his son Mongke are consistently flattered, while Ogodei is shown cursing Guyug for his cruelty and lack of respect for his elders. The Khan himself is even given a speech admitting faults such as disloyalty to a follower and excessive drinking. It seems likely that the author, of this section at least, was a member of Tolui's camp, and that the stories reflect the conflict that had already arisen between the families of Tolui and Ogodei before Ogodei's death in the winter of 1241/1242. Ogodei's wife, Doregene, and Guyug were to control the empire for the remainder of the decade. After Guyug also died of alcoholism in 1248, Tolui's sons were to take over. Mongke became the fourth Great Khan, and the last to rule over an administratively unified empire. His brother Khubilai (the Kubilai Khan of Marco Polo and Kubla Khan of Coleridge) succeeded Mongke after some conflict with the youngest of Tolui's sons, Arikh-bukha. Khubilai accomplished the final conquest and unification of China and established the Yuan Dynasty, which he ruled for over three decades. The third son, Hulegu, established the Il-khan dynasty in Persia after destroying the power of the Caliph and sacking Baghdad. When the thirteenth century began, Chingis Khan had sent his armies sweeping across all of Eurasia. By the end of that century, and well into the next, his grandchildren ruled it all. What had begun as a struggle for power within the tribes of Mongolia had remade the political and cultural arrangement of Eastern Europe, the Middle East, Central Asia, and China.

Mongolian landscapes

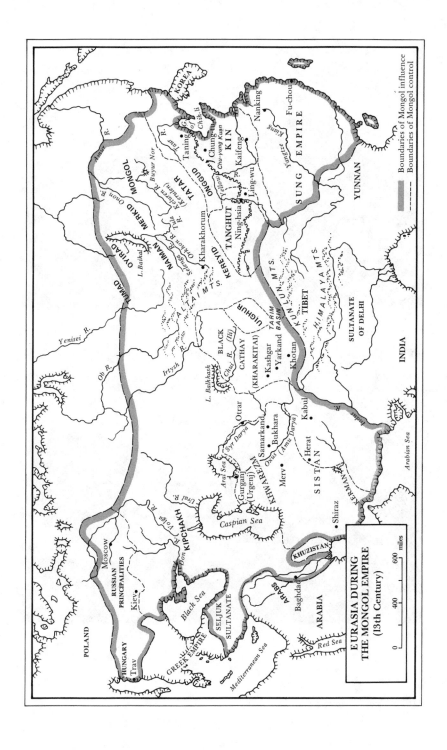

EURASIA DURING
THE MONGOL EMPIRE
(13th Century)

Boundaries of Mongol influence
Boundaries of Mongol control

0   400   600 miles

Mongolian landscapes

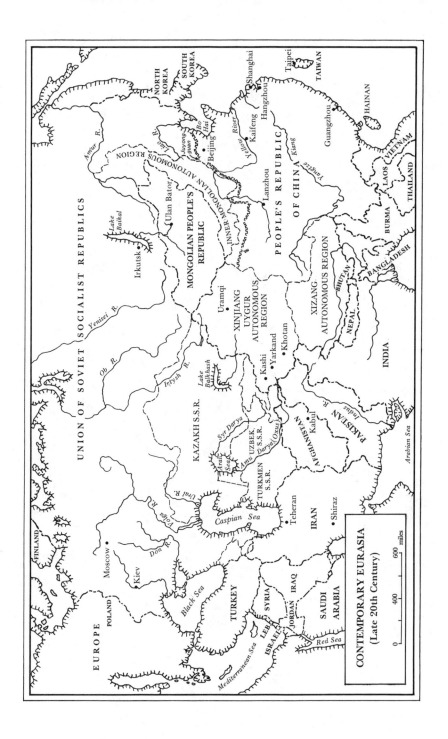

CONTEMPORARY EURASIA
(Late 20th Century)

THE SECRET HISTORY OF THE MONGOLS

The Origin of Chingis Khan

The Heritage and Youth of Chingis Khan

There came into the world a blue-gray wolf
whose destiny was Heaven's will.
His wife was a fallow deer.
They travelled together across the inland sea
and when they were camped near the source of the Onan River
in sight of Mount Burkhan Khaldun
their first son was born, named Batachikhan.

The seventh generation after Batachikhan was Kharchu.
Kharchu's son was named Borjigidai the Clever,
and Mongoljin the Fair was his wife.
Their grandsons were the two brothers,
Duua the Blind and Dobun the Clever.
In the middle of Duua's forehead there was one great eye.
With this eye Duua could see a place so far away
it could take three days to reach it.

One day Duua climbed up Mount Burkhan Khaldun with his younger brother.
Looking out from the mountain
Duua could see a band of people approaching,
driving their carts along the Tungelig Stream.
"In the middle of a band of people I see coming this way,
at the front of a black cart,
there's a fine-looking woman," he said.
"If she's not already promised in marriage
I'll ask that she be given to you," he said to his younger brother
and he sent Dobun down to meet her.
When Dobun reached the travelling camp
he saw she was indeed a good woman,

fine to look at with noble manners,
well known and respected by her own people,
given the name of Alan the Fair.
She hadn't yet been promised in marriage.
Long ago the Lord of Kol Barghuji Hollow
had given his daughter, Barghujin,
to a chief of the Khori Tuman clan, named Khorilartai the Clever.
Now this was their daughter we speak of,
who was born to Barghujin and Khorilartai
while they camped at the Arigh River
and they gave her the name of Alan the Fair.
After she was grown her father, Khorilartai, gathered his people together.
They'd been restricted from hunting by neighboring clans in the Khori Tumad country,
an area rich in sable, squirrel, and other wild game.
They left there and changed their clan name to Khorilar.
Khorilartai said to his people:
"The wild game of Mount Burkhan Khaldun is easy to hunt
and the land around the mountain is good grazing land."
They came to the territory of the Uriangkhai people,
whose leaders allowed them to settle.
This is how Duua came to ask for
and Dobun came to marry
Khorilartai's daughter, Alan the Fair.

So Alan the Fair came to live with Dobun
and she bore him two sons, named Bugunutei and Belgunutei.
Duua, the elder brother, had four sons,
and in time he passed away.
After Duua was gone his four sons wouldn't follow their uncle's authority.
They hated their uncle
so they took their own people away and made their own camp.
The four brothers took the clan name Dorbun, meaning 'the four'
and these were the first of the Dorbun people.
After they'd left him
their uncle Dobun went out hunting one day up in Tokhochagh Heights.
In the forest there he met with an Uriangkhai man
who'd just brought down a three-year-old deer

and was cooking its ribs on a fire.
  Dobun said to the hunter:
"My friend, give me the meat that you're cooking."
"Certainly, I'll give you the meat," the man answered him.
  He cut off half of the breast with the lungs,
  as well as the hide to keep for himself,
  then he gave Dobun all the rest of the deer meat.
  So Dobun set out carrying the meat from the deer on his horse,
  and on his way back he met with a poor man on foot
  leading his son by the hand.
"What people are you from?" Dobun asked him.
  The man replied:
"I am a Magaligh Bayagud, and I haven't had food for days.
  Give me some of that deer meat and I'll give you my son in return."
  Dobun accepted the man's offer.
  He broke off a thigh from the three-year-old deer
  and gave it to the hungry man.
  Then Dobun took the man's son back with him to work in his tent.
  In time Dobun passed away
  and after he was gone Alan the Fair, without a husband,
  gave birth to three more sons.
  They were named Bughu Khatagi, Bughutu Salji, and Bodonchar the Fool.
  The first two sons, Belgunutei and Bugunutei,
  talked to each other about this:
"Even though our mother has no brothers or kin here
  and now has no husband at all
  she's given birth to three sons.
  The only man in her tent is the servant,
  the boy our father brought from the Magaligh Bayagud.
  These three must be his children."
  Even though they were careful to say all this out of her sight,
  their mother, Alan, could hear them talking about her.
  Then one day in the spring,
  while boiling a soup from dried mutton,
  Alan the Fair assembled her five sons together.
  She seated them all in a row,
  gave them each the shaft of an arrow

and said to them: "Break it!"
A single arrow shaft,
it took no great strength to break it,
and each of them broke it and tossed it away.
Then she bound together five shafts in a bundle,
and giving the bundle to each in his turn,
said to each of them: "Break it!"
Each of the brothers held the five bound together
and no one could break them.
Then their mother, Alan, said to them:
"Belgunutei and Bugunutei,
you are my first two sons and you've doubted me.
You've said to each other:
'She's given birth to three new sons.
Who is their father and what is their clan?'
You're right to ask questions like this,
so I'll tell you.
Every night a man as yellow as the sun would enter my tent
by the light from the smoke-hole
or by the place light enters at the top of the door.
He'd rub on my belly.
The light from this man would sink into my womb.
Then he'd leave me,
crawling out on the sunbeams or the shafts of moonlight,
crawling up like a dog as yellow as the sun.
So now do you believe me?
Now that you know the truth can't you see it's a sign?
These brothers of yours must be the sons of Eternal Heaven.
How can you think these are the sons of a mortal man?
When they become Lords of all people,
then common men will understand who they are."
Then Alan the Fair spoke to her five sons and gave them this advice:
"You five were all born from one womb.
If, like the five single arrows that you held
you separate yourselves, each going alone,
then each of you can be broken by anyone.
If you are drawn together by a singular purpose

6

bound like the five shafts in a bundle
how can anyone break you?"

togetherness and necessity to stay together to avoid demise

Then in time Alan the Fair passed away.
After their mother, Alan, was gone
the five brothers divided among themselves the herd and the food.
Belgunutei, Bugunutei, Bughu Khatagi, and Bughutu Salji,
each of these four took an equal part.
Then looking at Bodonchar they said to each other:
"He's witless and a fool."
They wouldn't acknowledge him as their brother
and gave Bodonchar nothing at all.
When Bodonchar saw he'd been left out he said to himself:
"What'll I do with myself now?"
He saddled a grayish-white horse with a black stripe down its back,
with sores on its spine and no hair on its tail,
and said to himself:
"If my horse dies then I'll die.
If my horse lives then I'll live."
He set out riding down the Onan River till he reached Baljun Island.
There he fashioned himself a tent from the river grass to live in.
Then he saw a gray falcon that had killed a black pheasant
and was eating its prey not far from his tent.
Bodonchar fashioned a snare from the horse's tailhair,
from the grayish-white horse with a black stripe down its back,
with sores on its spine and no hair on its tail,
and he caught the young falcon.
He trained the bird to hunt food for them both.
When he was hungry
he'd find where the wolves had surrounded some game on a cliff,
then shooting down some of this game the wolves trapped for him
he'd feed himself and his falcon.
Then it was spring again.
As the ducks returned north
he starved his falcon and let the bird loose.
From tree branches he hung all the ducks and wild geese his falcon brought down.
There were so many birds

the smell of their flesh rose from every old tree,
the stink of spoiled meat came from every dead tree on the island.
Then from Mount Duyiren
a band of people came travelling down along Tungelig Stream.
Bodonchar would send out his falcon to hunt
then go to drink mare's milk at their camp all day
and return to his grass tent to sleep every night.
These people never asked Bodonchar:
"Who was your father and what is your clan?"
and Bodonchar never asked them:
"What people are you?"
Then that year Bughu Khatagi decided to search for his younger brother.
He thought to himself:
"We saw him set off down the Onan River,"
so he rode off that way
till he met the people who'd come travelling down along Tungelig Stream.
He asked them if they'd seen such and such a man
riding on such and such a horse.
The people told him:
"Both a man and a horse like the ones you describe have been here.
The man has a falcon.
Every day he comes to our camp,
drinks our mare's milk and then leaves.
We don't know where he spends the night.
But if the wind's from the northwest
our camp's hit by a blizzard of feathers and down thick as snow.
They must be from the geese and the ducks his falcon has killed.
So he must live nearby, over that way.
If you wait here a moment he'll probably show up."
And a few minutes later they saw a man riding toward them
riding along the Tungelig Stream.
When the man reached the camp he dismounted
and Bughu Khatagi saw it was his younger brother, Bodonchar.
He ordered his brother back on his horse,
and riding beside him, they trotted back along the Onan River.
Bodonchar just trotted along,
riding beside Bughu Khatagi and said to him:

"Elder brother, elder brother,
 it's a good thing when a body has a head.
 It's a good thing when a coat has a collar."
 His elder brother didn't even listen,
 so he repeated the same words again.
 His elder brother thought he was just talking nonsense and said nothing back.
 Bodonchar just trotted along
 and again he repeated the very same words.
 This time Bughu Khatagi turned to him and said:
"What's this that you're saying over and over?"
 And Bodonchar answered him:
"These people we've left at the Tungelig Stream
 they make no distinctions between the big and the little,
 the bad and the good,
 the head and the hoof.
 They all live like equals.
 With no leaders they'll be an easy group to take by surprise.
 Why don't we rob them?"
 Then his elder brother understood what he meant, and said:
"Well, if that's the case we'll go back to our tent.
 All five of us brothers will plan this together
 and then we'll attack them."
 When they got back to the tent all the brothers talked and set out together.
 They sent Bodonchar ahead of the rest to act as their spy.
 The first person Bodonchar met as he approached the camp was a pregnant woman.
 He captured her and asked her:
"What people do you come from?"
 She told him:
"I am an Uriangkhai from the Jarchigud clan."
 Then the five brothers attacked the camp
 and took for themselves all the cattle and food
 all the people and servants
 all the possessions and tents.

The woman Bodonchar captured
came to live in his tent and gave birth to a son.
Since he was the child of a foreign people

he was given the name Jajiradai, 'the foreigner.'
He was the first of the Jadaran clan and Jamugha's ancestor.
This same woman then had a son by Bodonchar.
Since the mother of the boy was a woman he'd captured
he named the boy Bagaridai, 'the captured one.'
He was the first of the Bagarin clan.
Bagaridai had a son named Chidukhul the Athlete
and Chidukhul had numerous wives who gave bith to numerous sons.
Since there were so many of them
they took Menen Bagarin as their clan name, 'the numerous captives.'
Now each of Alan the Fair's five sons was the first of a clan.
Bodonchar was the first of the Borjigin clan and Temujin's ancestor.
Bodonchar had a son by his first-ranking wife named Khabichi the Brave.
Khabichi had a son named Tumun the Numerous,
who had seven sons before he died.
His eldest was Khachi the Hero
who married Mother Nomolun,
and their son was Khaidu.
Khaidu was the first to rule all the Mongol
and he had three sons.
His eldest son, Shingkhor,
had a son Tumbinai, whose son was Khabul Khan.
The next son of Khaidu was Charakhai
whose son was Ambaghai Khan.
Ambaghai was the first of the Tayichigud clan.
Khabul Khan ruled after Khaidu was gone,
and he had seven sons.
The eldest was Okin Barkhagh
and his son was Sorkhatu Jurki,
first of the Jurkin clan.
Sorkhatu Jurki's two sons were Sacha Beki and Taichu.
The next son of Khabul Khan was Bartan the Brave
who had four sons.
His third son was Yesugei the Brave, Temujin's father.
The next son of Khabul was Khutughtu
whose son was Buri the Athlete.
This is the same Buri the Athlete

the one who stabbed Belgutei during the feast on the Onan.
The fourth son of Khabul was Khutula Khan
and Jochi and Altan were his sons.
Khabul Khan ruled all the Mongol
and when he passed away
even though he had seven sons of his own
he asked that his cousin, Ambaghai Khan, take the throne.
Then Ambaghai Khan gave his daughter in marriage to one of the Tatar clans,
the Tatar who lived on the Urshun River
between Lake Buyur and Lake Kolen.
As he rode through that country to deliver his daughter
he was seized by another Tatar clan
and taken in chains to the Golden King of Cathay.
When he was captured
Ambaghai Khan sent one of his men back with a message.
He told the messenger:
"You'll speak to Khutula, middle son of Khabul Khan,
and of my ten sons you'll speak with Khadagan Taisi.
Tell them,
'Beware of the Tatar and don't forget what they've done to me.
When you become Lord of all men
don't forget that I was betrayed by the Tatar,
dragged off in chains as I brought them my daughter to marry.
You must try to avenge me with all the strength you can find,
till the nails of your fingers wear off,
till your fingers themselves wear away from your hands!' "

That year Yesugei the Brave was out hunting with his falcon on the Onan.
Yeke Chiledu, a nobleman of the Merkid tribe,
had gone to the Olkhunugud people to find himself a wife,
and he was returning to the Merkid with the girl he'd found
when he passed Yesugei hunting by the river.
When he saw them riding along Yesugei leaned forward on his horse.
He saw it was a beautiful girl.
Quickly he rode back to his tent
and just as quick returned with his two brothers,
Nekun Taisi and Daritai Odchigin.

When Chiledu saw the three Mongol coming
he whipped his dun-colored horse
and rode off around a nearby hill with the three men behind him.
He cut back around the far side of the hill
and rode back to Hogelun Ujin, the girl he'd just married,
who stood waiting for him at the front of their cart.
"Did you see the look on the faces of those three men?" she asked him.
"From their faces it looks like they mean to kill you.
As long as you've got your life
there'll always be girls for you to choose from.
There'll always be women to ride in your cart.
As long as you've got your life
you'll be able to find some girl to marry.
When you find her,
just name her Hogelun for me,
but go now and save your own life!"
Then she pulled off her shirt and held it out to him, saying:
"And take this to remember me,
to remember my scent."
Chiledu reached out from his saddle and took the shirt in his hands.
With the three Mongol close behind him
he struck his dun colored horse with his whip
and took off down the Onan River at full speed.
The three Mongol chased him across seven hills
before turning around and returning to Hogelun's cart.
Then Yesugei the Brave grasped the reins of the cart,
his elder brother Nekun Taisi rode in front to guide them,
and the younger brother Daritai Odchigin rode along by the wheels.
As they rode her back toward their camp,
Hogelun began to cry, saying:
"My young master Chiledu has never had to set his face into the wind.
He's never had to ride hungry across desert lands.
And now you've made him run for his life,
riding into the wind.
He looks ahead,
and the wind tosses his two braids of hair onto his back.
He turns to look back,

and the braids are tossed onto his breast.
The wind tosses them forward,
then tosses them back
as he rides alone across desert lands."
Then she set up a loud wailing,
and she cried till she stirred up the waters of the Onan River,
till she shook the trees in the forest and the grass in the valleys.
But as the party approached their camp
Daritai, riding beside her, warned her to stop:
"This fellow who held you in his arms,
he's already ridden over the mountains.
This man who's lost you,
he's crossed many rivers by now.
You can call out his name,
but he can't see you now even if he looks back.
If you tried to find him now
you won't even find his tracks.
So be still now," he told her.
Then Yesugei took Hogelun Ujin to his tent as his wife.

Since the last message Ambaghai Khan sent
had named both his son Khadagan and his nephew Khutula,
all the Mongol and Tayichigud people gathered in the Khorkhonagh Valley for a Great Assembly.
They decided to make Khutula their new ruler
and this set the Mongol to dancing and feasting.
Once they made Khutula their khan
they danced around the Great Branching Tree of Khorkhonagh,
dancing until they'd beaten down a ditch as deep as their waist,
dancing until they'd raised up the dust as high as their knees.

So Khutula Khan and Khadagan went to war with the Tatar.
Thirteen times they met each other in battle
but they weren't able to get their revenge.
They weren't able to get satisfaction for Ambaghai Khan's death.
It was during one of these battles
that Yesugei captured a Tatar chief named Temujin Uge.
Yesugei's people were camped at Deligun Hill on the Onan then,

and Hogelun Ujin was about to give birth to her first child.
It was here that Chingis Khan was born.
As he was born
he emerged clutching a blood clot the size of a knucklebone die in his right hand.
They gave him the name Temujin, saying:
"He was born when his father had captured the Tatar, Temujin Uge."
Yesugei had four sons by Hogelun Ujin,
Temujin, Khasar, Khachigun, and Temuge.
Then they had one daughter, Temulun.
When Temujin was nine years old
Khasar was seven and Alchidai Khachigun was five.
Temuge Odchigin was only three and Temulun was still in the cradle.

That year, when Temujin was nine,
Yesugei decided to take him to visit his mother's tribe, saying:
"I'll ask for a girl from his mother's tribe to marry him."
On their way to the Olkhunugud tribe they met an Ungirad man, Dei the Wise,
camped between Mount Chegcher and Mount Chikhurkhu.
Dei the Wise addressed Yesugei as if they were related by marriage:
"My friend Yesugei, travelling so far,
who are you going to see?"
"I'm on my way to the Olkhunugud,
the tribe of this son of mine's mother,
to find a girl for him there," he replied.
Dei the Wise said to him:
"I look at your son and I see
his eyes contain fire,
his face fills with light.
My friend Yesugei, I had a dream last night.
A white falcon holding the Sun and the Moon in its claws
flew down from the sky and lit on my hand.
I told my family this, saying:
'Whenever I saw the Sun or the Moon in my dreams before
it was always from a distance.
Now this falcon, taking them in his claws,
has brought them both into my hand.
The bird was all white and it brought them to me.

What does this good omen mean?' I asked.

My friend Yesugei,

I had this dream the very moment you were leading your son to our camp.

What could it mean?

Obviously it was a sign that a nobleman like yourself would come to our camp.

Since the days of old we Ungirad have been protected by the beauty of our daughters,

by the loveliness of our granddaughters,

and so we've stayed out of battles and wars.

When you elect a new khan,

we take our loveliest daughters and place them on carts.

Harnessing a black camel to the cart,

we have him trot off to the khan's tent.

We offer our daughters to sit there beside him and be his khatun.

We don't challenge empires;

we don't go to war with our neighbors.

We just bring up our daughters and place them in the front of the carts.

Harnessing a black camel to the cart,

we lead them off to the khan's tent.

We offer our daughters to sit by the khan,

and he places them up on the throne.

Since the days of old the Ungirad have had khatun as their shields.

We've survived by the loveliness of our granddaughters,

by the beauty of our daughters.

When one of our boys wants to marry

you can judge the wealth of our camp to decide if you want him.

But as for our girls you only have to look at their beauty.

My friend Yesugei, let's go to my tent.

I've got a young daughter there.

My friend should meet her."

Dei the Wise led Yesugei's horse to his tent and helped him dismount.

When Yesugei saw Dei's daughter he was impressed.

She was a girl whose face filled with light,

whose eyes filled with fire,

and he began to consider her father's proposal.

She was ten years old, a year older than Temujin,

and her name was Borte.

After spending the night in the tent,

the next morning Yesugei asked Dei for his daughter.
"I could let you have her after awhile,
  waiting for you to ask me again and again,
  but who'd praise me for stalling?
  I could let you have her right away,
  just waiting for you to ask me twice,
  and who'd curse me for replying too quick?
  No, this girl's fate is not to grow old by the door of the tent she was born in.
  I'll be happy to give you my daughter.
  But now you should go,
  and leave your son with me for awhile,
  so we can get to know our new son-in-law."
Both men gave their pledge to the other
and Yesugei added:
"I'll leave you my son for awhile.
  You should know that he's frightened by dogs.
  Don't let the dogs frighten him, my friend."
Then Yesugei offered his lead horse as a gift,
and leaving Temujin in Dei's tent, he rode back to his people.

As he rode back Yesugei came on a camp of the Tatar,
  who were feasting below Mount Chegcher on the Yellow Steppe.
  Tired and thirsty, he dismounted to join in the feasting.
  But the Tatar recognized who he was, and said to themselves:
"Yesugei of the Kiyan clan is among us here."
  They remembered the times he'd defeated them in battle.
  Secretly they decided to kill him,
  mixing poisons into the drinks he was offered.
  On his way back he felt something was wrong
  and after riding three days to get back to his tent
  he knew he was dying.
Yesugei the Brave spoke from his bed, saying:
"I feel that I'm dying.
  Who's here beside me?"
Someone answered him:
"Munglig, the son of Old Man Charakha is here."
  Yesugei called the boy over to him and said:

16

"Munglig, my child, my sons are still very young.
  As I rode back from leaving Temujin with his wife's family
  I was secretly poisoned by the Tatar.
  I can feel that I'm dying now.
  Take care of my sons like they were your own little brothers.
  Take care of my wife like she was your own elder sister.
  Go quickly now, Munglig, my child, and bring Temujin back."
  Then Yesugei passed away.
  Following Yesugei's last words Munglig went to Dei the Wise and said:
"My Elder Brother Yesugei's heart aches
  and he is constantly thinking of his son.
  I've come to take Temujin back to him."
  Dei the Wise answered him:
"If my friend thinks so much of his son, I'll let him go.
  When he's seen his father again, have him quickly come back."
  So Father Munglig brought Temujin back to his family.

The following spring Ambaghai's widows, Orbei and Sokhatai,
  the senior women of the Tayichigud clan,
  performed the ceremony of sacrifice to the ancestor's spirits.
  By the time Hogelun Ujin arrived for the service
  they'd already burnt all the meat
  and divided it between them, leaving her nothing.
  Hogelun said to them:
"You must be saying to yourselves,
  'Yesugei the Brave is dead now and his sons are still boys.'
  So you think you can just leave me out of the ceremony
  and keep it all for yourselves?
  You think you can divide up the meats and leave nothing for me?
  I see what you're up to.
  You think that I'll just sit here while you're feasting from now on,
  that you don't even have to invite me to join you.
  And one morning you'll break camp and move on,
  and not even wake me."
  Orbei and Sokhatai, the two old khatun, answered her:
"Obviously you live by some rule that says,
  'I don't need to be offered some food before I take something to eat.'

You have the custom of eating whatever you can find.
You seem to have a rule that says,
'I don't need to be invited to take part in a feast.'
Your custom is to just come uninvited and take for yourself.
Tell us, Hogelun, do you say to yourself,
'Ambaghai Khan is dead now,'
is that why you think you can insult us this way?"
Later the old women conferred among themselves and said:
"The best thing to do is abandon these people,
these mothers and sons.
We should break camp and leave them behind."

So at dawn the next day the two chiefs of the Tayichigud clan,
Targhutai Kiriltugh and Todogen Girte,
ordered the people to move on down the Onan River.
Old Man Charakha saw they were leaving Hogelun Ujin behind,
that they were abandoning these mothers and sons,
so he stepped forward, protesting to Todogen Girte.
But Todogen said to him:
"Everything has changed now.
The deepest waters are dry,
the brightest gem has been broken to pieces,"
and the chief ordered the people to keep moving along.
Then when Old Man Charakha turned away from him
Todogen yelled back:
"What gives you the right to say that we're wrong to do this?"
and he drove a spear into the old man's back.
Old Man Charakha struggled back to his tent
and lay down in great pain from his wound.
Temujin came to his bedside and the old man said to him:
"As the Tayichigud were taking the people your good father assembled,
as they were taking our people away from the camp,
I stepped out and protested to Todogen.
See what he's done to me."
Temujin sat and wept by the dying man
and then left the tent.

When Hogelun Ujin saw the people were leaving her
she grabbed up the standard of Yesugei the Brave
and rode out into the travelling camp.
Just the sight of her holding the banner
and shouting caused half of the people to stop and turn back with her.
But the ones who turned back couldn't stay.
They were forced to return with the others by the Tayichigud
and told to move on.
After the Tayichigud brothers had abandoned the old camp,
leaving only Hogelun Ujin,
her sons and her little ones,
after the Tayichigud had taken all of the people away,
leaving only the mothers and sons,
Hogelun Ujin, a woman born with great power,
took care of her sons.
Proudly she put on her headdress and gathered the folds of her skirt.
She went up and down the banks of the Onan
and gathered pears and wild fruit.
Day and night she found food for their mouths.
Mother Hogelun, a woman born with great courage,
took care of her sons.
Taking a juniper stick in her hands
she fed them by digging up roots.
These boys who were nourished on the wild onion and pear,
who were fed by Ujin, the Mother,
became the great Lords of all men.
These boys who lived on the roots that she dug for them,
who were cared for with pride by Mother Ujin,
became the wise men who gave us our laws.
These boys who were nourished on the wild onion and pear,
who were fed by the beautiful Ujin,
grew up to be fine, daring men.
Once they'd grown into men,
they pledged to themselves: "Now we'll feed our mother."
They sat on the banks of the Mother Onan
and bent needles they'd found into fishhooks.
With these hooks they caught a few misshapen fish.

They made nets to sweep through the river
and they caught tiny fish.
With these in their turn they helped feed their mother.

One day Temujin and Khasar,
along with their half-brothers Begter and Belgutei,
were sitting together on the riverbank
pulling a hook through the water
when they saw a shiny fish had been caught on it.
When they landed the fish
Begter and Belgutei took it away from Temujin and Khasar.
Temujin and Khasar ran back to their tent to complain to Mother Ujin:
"Begter and Belgutei took a fish from us,
a shiny fish that bit on our hook."
But even though Begter and Belgutei were only her stepsons
Mother Ujin replied:
"Stop this!
How can brothers act this way with each other?
Now, when we've no one to fight beside us but our own shadows,
when there's nothing to whip our horses but their own tails,
how will we get our revenge on the Tayichigud brothers?
Why do you fight among yourselves like the five sons of Mother Alan?
Don't be this way."
But Temujin and Khasar wouldn't listen to what she said.
They ignored her warning and answered instead:
"Besides that, yesterday they took a bird from us,
a lark we'd shot down with one of our own arrows.
And now they've stolen a fish.
How can we live with them?"
The two boys pushed aside the door of the tent and stalked out.
While Begter sat in a clearing watching the family's nine horses grazing,
Temujin hid himself in the grass and crept up from behind
while Khasar crept up from the front.
Then suddenly they sprang up,
drawing their arrows to shoot,
and Begter, seeing what they meant to do to him, said:
"How can you do this to me,

when our mouths are filled
with the bitterness of what the Tayichigud clan has done,
when we ask ourselves,
'How can we get our revenge on them?'
how can you treat me like some dirt in your eye,
like something that's keeping the food from your mouth?
How can you do this,
when there's no one to fight beside us but our own shadows,
when there's nothing to whip our horses but their own tails,
how can you kill me?
But if you must
don't destroy the fire of my hearth.
Don't kill my brother Belgutei too!"
Then Begter sat down before them,
crossing his legs,
and waited to see what they'd do to him.
At close range both Temujin and Khasar shot arrows into him,
striking him down in the front and the back,
and then left him.
When they got back to the tent
Mother Ujin could see on their faces what they'd done.
She looked at her two sons,
then pointing first at Temujin said to them:
"Killers, both of you!
When he came out screaming from the heat of my womb
this one was born holding a clot of black blood in his hand.
And now you've both destroyed without thinking,
like the Khasar dog who eats its own afterbirth,
like the panther that heedlessly leaps from a cliff,
like the lion who can't control its own fury,
like the python that thinks: 'I'll swallow my prey alive,'
like the falcon that foolishly dives at its own shadow,
like the river pike who silently swallows the smaller fish,
like the he-camel who snaps at the heels of his colt,
like the wolf who hides himself in the blizzard to hunt down his prey,
like the mandarin duck who eats his own chicks when they fall behind,
like the jackal who fights with anyone who's touched him,

like the tiger who doesn't think before seizing his prey,
you've killed your own brother!
When we have no one to fight beside us but our own shadows,
when there's nothing to whip our horses with but their own tails,
when our mouths are filled
with the bitterness of what the Tayichigud have done to us,
and we ask ourselves:
'How can we get our revenge on them?'
you come complaining to me, saying:
'How can we live with these brothers?'
and now you do this!"
This is how she spoke to her sons,
reciting ancient phrases and quoting old sayings to them in her anger.

Targhutai Kiriltugh, the Tayichigud chief, said to himself:
"Hogelun's brood must have molted by now.
Her droolers must have grown into little men."
He gathered some of his soldiers and rode back down the river to find them.
When the family saw the soldiers approaching they were frightened.
The mother and her children,
young ones and old ones,
built a quick fortress in the woods.
Belgutei pulled down small trees to fashion a barricade
and Khasar fired off a volley of arrows to hold the soldiers back.
While these two older boys fought
Hogelun took Khadigun, Temuge, and Temulun
and she hid them in the opening of a nearby cliff.
Then the Tayichigud shouted to them:
"Send out your elder brother, Temujin.
We're not here to fight with you.
We're here to get him."
But the Tayichigud realized that Temujin had escaped them.
He'd slipped out and run for the woods with his horse.
They pursued him until he reached the woods at the top of Mount Tergune.
Then they stopped there
since the forest was too thick to ride into
and the Tayichigud stood watch at the entrance

waiting for Temujin to come out.
Temujin hid in the woods for three nights
then said to himself:
"Now I'll escape."
But as he led out his horse
his saddle seemed to fall off by itself.
He went back to where the saddle had fallen and looked at it closely.
The breast strap was still buckled and the belly cinch was in place,
yet somehow it fell off the horse.
He said to himself:
"The belly cinch could stay fastened and it could still slip back,
but how could a breast strap come off without coming unbuckled?
I think Heaven wants me to stay here."
So he returned to his hiding place and spent three more nights.
Then again he tried to escape
but as he neared the edge of the forest
a white boulder the size of a tent
fell down in the path and blocked the way out.
He said to himself:
"I think Heaven wants me to stay here,"
and for three more nights he stayed in the woods.
For nine nights now he'd been without food
and he said to himself:
"I don't want to die here, forgotten and nameless.
I've got to escape."
He cut a new path around the boulder
using the knife he carried to cut himself arrows.
The brush was so thick there
he couldn't push through until he'd hacked a new path.
But as he led his horse out the Tayichigud were still waiting.
They captured him there and took him away.

Targhutai Kiriltugh had Temujin taken back to his camp as a prisoner,
ordering that he be passed around from tent to tent,
spending one night in each tent.
On the sixteenth day of the summer's first moon,
the Red Circle Day of that year,

the Tayichigud held a big feast on the banks of the Onan.

By twilight the people began to disperse.

A weak little fellow had been given the job of guarding Temujin that day,

and when all the people had passed out or gone home

Temujin yanked his cangue away from his guard.

He swung the wood collar around and hit his guard once in the head with it,

then ran for the river as fast as he could.

He thought to himself:

"If I run for the woods they'll spot me there,"

so he went to the river,

and using his cangue as a float,

he lay back in the river with only his face sticking out of the water.

When the fellow he'd beaten came to, he yelled:

"I've lost him! Temujin's escaped!"

When they heard that

all the Tayichigud who had gone back to their tents

came out to search for him.

It was the night of full moon

and the moonlight was bright as the day.

Most went to look in the forest

thinking that's where he'd run.

But as Sorkhan Shira passed by the river

he saw Temujin lying there and said to him quietly:

"It's because you're a clever young man that the Tayichigud are afraid of you.

They say that your eyes contain fire,

that your face fills with light.

Just stay where you are.

I won't tell them I've seen you,"

and he kept right on pretending to search.

When they all came back to the feasting grounds someone said:

"Let's search again."

Sorkhan Shira spoke up, saying:

"Yes, let's go back again.

Each of us go back to the place we just searched and look again."

They agreed and went back to the same places,

and as Sorkhan Shira passed by the river, he whispered to Temujin:

"They're still after you.

Don't move yet."

They came back to the feasting ground and again someone said:

"Let's go back and search for him more."

And Sorkhan Shira spoke up this time, saying:

"My Tayichigud leaders, you've lost a man in broad daylight.

How can you expect to find him at night?

Let's look in the same places once more,

then go back to our tents.

Tomorrow we'll gather again and we'll find him.

How far can he go with a cangue on his neck?"

All agreed and went back to searching one last time for the night.

As Sorkhan Shira passed Temujin's hiding place he whispered:

"They said, 'Let's search one more time.

Then we'll go back to our tents and search tomorrow again.'

Lie quiet until they've gone away.

And don't tell anyone about this.

If you're captured don't tell them I saw you."

Temujin lay still in the water

waiting until all the men had gone back to their tents.

He tried to figure out what to do next,

and looking into his heart he thought:

"As I was passed from family to family,

from tent to tent,

I was taken to the tent of Sorkhan Shira.

His sons Chimbai and Chilagun were kind to me.

They even took the cangue off my neck

so I could sleep one night without it.

Now it's Sorkhan Shira who found me but didn't let them know.

Maybe that family will save me."

He pulled himself out of the river

and went off to find Sorkhan Shira's tent.

Temujin knew that their's was the tent where the kumis was made.

During the day the leather jars were filled with mare's milk,

then all night they would beat the jars till the milk had fermented to kumis.

He found their tent by listening in the dark for the sound of the beater.

As he slipped in the door,

Sorkhan Shira cried out in a hushed voice:

"What are you doing here?
  Didn't I tell you, 'Go find your mother and brothers'?"
  But his sons, Chimbai and Chilagun, protested, saying:
"If a falcon chases a sparrow into a bush,
  then the bush saves the sparrow.
  Now that he's here you can't throw him out."
  They wouldn't listen to their father,
  and removing Temujin's cangue,
  they burnt it up in the fireplace.
  They had him hide in a cart full of wool
  and ordered their sister, Khadagan, to take care of him, telling her:
"Don't let anyone know that he's here."
  After searching for him three days the Tayichigud leaders said:
"Someone in camp must be hiding him.
  Let's search all the tents."
  They came to Sorkhan Shira's tent and began searching everything.
  They went through his chests,
  through his carts,
  even looking under his beds.
  Finally they came to the cart filled with wool,
  and began throwing the wool on the floor,
  approaching the back of the cart.
"How could anyone survive all the heat,
  buried under so much wool?" Sorkhan Shira said to the searchers,
  and they looked at him,
  looked at the wool,
  threw it back in the cart and left.
  Once they'd gone Temujin came out from under the wool.
  Sorkhan Shira looked at him and said:
"You almost got us all killed,
  blown away like the ashes.
  Now get out of here.
  Go find your mother and brothers."
  He gave Temujin a straw-yellow mare,
  a barren one with a white mouth.
  He boiled him a fat lamb who'd been fed by two ewes,
  and gave him two leather buckets of kumis to drink.

26

He gave him no saddle nor flint to light fires,
and gave a bow with only two arrows.
This was to make sure that Temujin wouldn't stop to hunt on the way back.
Giving him these things and no more,
Sorkhan Shira told Temujin to leave.
Temujin rode without stopping
till he came to the place where his brothers had thrown up their fortress.
Reading their tracks in the grass,
he followed them up the banks of the Onan.
The Kimurgha River enters the Onan from the west there,
and he saw they'd gone up that way.
He found their new camp up this river near Khorchukhui Hill.
He rejoined his family and they moved camp again.
This time they went to Blue Lake
below Mount Khara Jirugen in the Sengur River valley.
There in the Gurelgu mountains,
in sight of Mount Burkhan Khaldun,
they lived on the marmots and field mice they caught.

Then one day thieves drove off the family's eight horses,
their silver-white geldings that grazed in front of their tent.
Temujin and his brothers could only watch the thieves ride away.
They had no horses left to chase after them.
Belgutei had taken their ninth horse that morning to hunt marmots,
the old straw-yellow mare with the hairless tail.
As the sun set that day
Belgutei came back leading the old mare on foot.
On the horse's back was a load of marmots he'd caught,
which swung to and fro as the horse walked along.
As he came into the camp he heard them yell:
"Thieves took our horses!"
"I'll go after them," Belgutei said.
  Khasar said, "No, you can't do it. I'll go."
"No, you won't. I'll go," Temujin said.
  He saddled the mare
  and followed the tracks that the geldings had left in the grass.
  After riding three nights

on the fourth morning he came on a huge herd.
A good-looking young man was tending the herd and milking the mares.
Temujin stopped and asked him if he'd seen the silver-white geldings,
and the fellow replied:
"Just this morning before sunrise
some men drove eight horses by here.
They sound like the ones you're after.
I'll show you their tracks."
He had Temujin put the mare out to pasture
and gave him a new horse to ride,
a grayish-white horse with a black stripe down its back.
Then the man saddled a fast dun-colored horse for himself.
Without even going back to his tent
he took his leather bucket and milk pail
and hid them right there in the grass.
"You look like you're in trouble," he said,
"the kind of trouble that can happen to any of us.
I'll go with you and be your companion.
My father is Nakhu the Rich and I'm his only son.
My name is Bogorchu."
So the two young men rode off together,
following the tracks in the grass.
They rode for three nights
then on the fourth day,
just as the sun was hitting the line of the hills,
they came to a large camping circle of tents.
They could see the eight silver-white geldings
grazing at one edge of the circle.
"Those are my horses," Temujin said when he saw them.
"You stay here, my friend.
I'll ride into the camp and drive them back this way."
But Bogorchu objected:
"I came with you to be your companion,
not stay here and watch."
So together they rode into the camp circle and drove out the horses.
The men of the camp
one after another
leaped to their horses and chased them.

One man on a white horse
  holding out a lasso pole
  began to close in behind them.
"Hand me the bow and some arrows," Bogorchu yelled,
"and I'll hold him off."
"No," Temujin said,
"I can't have you hurt for my sake.
  I'll stop him,"
  and he pulled up his horse and took aim.
  When the man with the lasso saw this
  he stopped and the others pulled up behind him.
  But the sun had set and the light disappeared.
  In the darkness Temujin and Bogorchu lost their pursuers.
  They rode for three days and three nights
  until they got back to Bogorchu's herd.
  Temujin said to him:
"My friend, could I have brought back these horses without you?
  Let's divide them between us.
  How many do you want?"
  But Bogorchu replied:
"When I saw you were in trouble I said,
  'I'll be your friend and I'll help you.'
  Should I take your horses now like they were my spoils?
  My father is called Nakhu the Rich
  and I am his only son.
  What my father will give me is all I need.
  If I've been any help that's my payment.
  I don't want your horses."
  Then they went back to Bogorchu's tent.
  Nakhu the Rich, thinking Bogorchu was dead, was in tears.
  When he saw the two young men coming
  and saw that one was his son,
  first he turned one way laughing
  then the other way crying.
"What's the matter with you?"
  Bogorchu said to his father.
"This man was in trouble.
  I decided I'd go be his friend and help out.

And now I've come back."
Bogorchu rode back to the herd
and fetched the leather bucket and milk pail,
the ones that he'd hidden in the grass six days before.
Then for Temujin he killed a fat lamb who'd been fed by two ewes,
and filled up a leather bucket with mare's milk.
Bogorchu gave him these provisions for his trip back to his family.
Then Nakhu the Rich said to them:
"You two boys are companions now.
From now on
the one should never abandon the other."
Temujin mounted his horse and rode for three days
till he got back to his camp on the Sengur River.
Mother Hogelun, Khasar, and the others were afraid he'd been lost,
but when they saw him ride in with the horses
they were happy again.

Ever since he was nine years old
when he'd first been promised in marriage to Borte Ujin,
Temujin planned to claim the daughter of Dei the Wise as his wife.
Now he took Belgutei
and together the brothers rode up the Keluren River to find her.
Dei the Wise still had a camp
on the plain between Mount Chegcher and Chikhurkhu.
When Temujin arrived there Dei was happy to see him.
"I'd heard that the Tayichigud leaders envied you," he said,
"and I'd almost given up hope of seeing you again.
But at last you've come back."
Dei the Wise gave him Borte
and together the family rode back toward Temujin's camp.
Dei the Wise accompanied them
as far as the place on the river called Uragh Chol.
Borte's mother, Chotan, rode all the way back to the Sengur River
where Temujin's people were camped.

After Chotan went back to her husband, Dei the Wise,
Temujin sent Belgutei to invite Bogorchu to join them.

As soon as Bogorchu got Temujin's message
he saddled a straw-yellow horse,
he tied his gray cloak behind the saddle,
and without even telling his father
he rode off with Belgutei.
From that time on Bogorchu was always at Temujin's side.

They moved their camp from the Sengur River
to the source of the Keluren,
at the base of a cliff called the Burgi.
Chotan had brought them a black sable coat as a wedding gift.
Now Temujin, Khasar, and Belgutei took this coat and rode off.
They remembered that long ago
Toghoril Ong Khan of the Kereyid had been anda with their father, Yesugei.
And Temujin said to himself:
"Since he was my father's anda then he's like my father."
So they rode to Ong Khan
who was camped near the Black Forest on the Tula River.
When they arrived at his camp
Temujin made a speech to Ong Khan:
"Since in the old days you and my father were anda
you're like my father.
I've just married an Ungirad woman
and I've brought you the wedding gift."
Then Temujin gave him the black sable coat.
Ong Khan was so pleased by this he promised Temujin:
"In return for this coat of sables
I'll get back all your people who've scattered.
In return for this coat of sables
I'll round up all your people who've gone separate ways.
Let my promise live here," he said,
touching his back,
"and here,"
touching his breast with his hand.
This done, the brothers rode back to their camp at Burgi.

And out of the mountains came an Uriangkhai man to join them.
It was Old Man Jarchigudai, the blacksmith,
with his bellows on his back.
He came to their camp leading Jelme, his son, and said:
"When your people were camped at Deligun Hill on the Onan,
when Temujin was born,
I gave you a sable blanket to swaddle the baby in.
I also gave you my son, Jelme,
but since he was just an infant then I kept him with me.
Now Jelme is yours,
to put on your saddle,
to open your door."
And he gave Temujin his son Jelme.

Their camp was still below Burgi
at the Keluren River's source,
when one morning just before dawn Old Woman Khogaghchin,
Mother Hogelun's servant,
woke with a start, crying:
"Mother! Mother! Get up!
The ground is shaking,
I hear it rumble.
The Tayichigud must be riding back to attack us.
Get up!"
Mother Hogelun jumped from her bed, saying:
"Quick, wake my sons!"
They woke Temujin and the others
and all ran for the horses.
Temujin, Mother Hogelun, and Khasar each took a horse.
Khachigun, Temuge Odchigin, and Belgutei each took a horse.
Bogorchu took one horse and Jelme another.
Mother Hogelun lifted the baby Temulun onto her saddle.
They saddled the last horse as a lead
and there was no horse left for Borte Ujin.
Temujin and his family rode out of the camp before daybreak,
toward the forests of Mount Burkhan Khaldun.

Old Woman Khogaghchin, who'd been left in the camp, said:
"I'll hide Borte Ujin."
She made her get into a black covered cart.
Then she harnessed the cart to a speckled ox.
Whipping the ox,
she drove the cart away from the camp down the Tungelig.
As the first light of day hit them,
soldiers rode up and told them to stop.
"Who are you?" they asked her,
and Old Woman Khogaghchin answered:
"I'm a servant of Temujin's.
I've just come from shearing his sheep.
I'm on my way back to my own tent to make felt from the wool."
Then they asked her:
"Is Temujin at his tent?
How far is it from here?"
Old Woman Khogaghchin said:
"As for the tent, it's not far.
As for Temujin, I couldn't see whether he was there or not.
I was just shearing his sheep out back."
The soldiers rode off toward the camp,
and Old Woman Khogaghchin whipped the ox.
But as the cart moved faster its axletree snapped.
"Now we'll have to run for the woods on foot," she thought,
but before she could start the soldiers returned.
They'd made Belgutei's mother their captive,
had her slung over one of their horses with her feet swinging down.
They rode up to the old woman shouting:
"What have you got in that cart!"
"I'm just carrying wool," Khogaghchin replied,
but an old soldier turned to the younger ones and said:
"Get off your horses and see what's in there."
When they opened the door of the cart they found Borte inside.
Pulling her out,
they forced Borte and Khogaghchin to ride on their horses,
then they all set out after Temujin

following his tracks in the grass,
riding at top speed toward Mount Burkhan Khaldun.
Three times around Mount Burkhan Khaldun they chased Temujin,
but they still couldn't catch him.
They rode this way and that through the thickets and swamps,
through a forest so dense that a snake could barely slip through it,
and though they could follow his trail
they couldn't catch up with him.
The men who pursued Temujin were the chiefs of the three Merkid clans,
Toghtoga, Dayir Usun, and Khagatai Darmala.
These three had come to get their revenge, saying:
"Long ago Mother Hogelun was stolen from our brother, Chiledu."
When they couldn't catch Temujin they said to each other:
"We've got our revenge.
We've taken their wives from them,"
and they rode down from Mount Burkhan Khaldun
back to their homes.
"Are the three Merkid actually gone,
or are they waiting out there to ambush us?" Temujin asked.
He sent Belgutei, Bogorchu, and Jelme down the mountain
and they trailed the Merkid for three days
to be sure they weren't coming back.
When he knew they were gone,
Temujin brought his family down from the mountain.
Sadly striking his breast with his hand, he spoke:
"Thanks to Mother Khogaghchin,
who hears like a weasel and sees like an ermine,
I've escaped with my life.
Leading my horse down the deer-paths,
making my tent from the elm branches,
I went up Mount Burkhan.
Though it seemed I'd be crushed like a louse
I escaped to Mount Burkhan Khaldun.
The mountain has saved my life and my horse.
Leading my horse down the elk-paths,
making my tent from the willow branches,
I went up Mount Burkhan.

34

Though I was frightened and ran like an insect,
I was shielded by Mount Burkhan Khaldun.
Every morning I'll offer a sacrifice to Mount Burkhan.
Every day I'll pray to the mountain.
Let my children and my children's children remember this."
Temujin turned toward the Sun and took his hat in his hand.
He loosened his belt and threw it over his neck.
Then striking his breast with his hand,
he knelt nine times to the Sun,
sprinkling offerings of mare's milk in the air,
and he prayed.

Having finished his prayer
Temujin rose and rode off with Khasar and Belgutei.
They rode to Toghoril Ong Khan of the Kereyid
camped in the Black Forest on the Tula River.
Temujin spoke to Ong Khan, saying:
"I was attacked by surprise by the three Merkid chiefs.
They've stolen my wife from me.
We've come to you now to say,
'Let my father the Khan save my wife and return her.'"
And Toghoril Ong Khan answered him:
"What did I say to you last year?
When you brought me the sable coat
when you wrapped me in it you said,
'Since in the old days you and my father were anda
you're like my father.'
And didn't I say to you,
'In return for this coat of sables
I'll get back all your people who've scattered.
In return for this coat of sables
I'll round up all your people who've gone separate ways'?
Didn't I say to you,
'Let my promise live here,'
touching my breast,
'and let it live here,'
touching my back?

I'll keep this promise I made for the coat
even if it means destroying the Merkid.
I'll rescue your Borte Ujin.
In return for the coat I'd even defeat all of the Merkid
and together we'll bring back your Khatun Borte.
First you send a messenger off to Younger Brother Jamugha.
I hear that he's camped in the Khorkhonagh Valley.
I'll start out from here with a force of twenty thousand soldiers
and be the Right Hand of the army.
Tell Younger Brother Jamugha to start out with twenty thousand as well
and be the Left Hand.
Let Jamugha decide when and where we should meet."
So when Temujin, Khasar, and Belgutei got back to their camp,
Temujin sent Khasar and Belgutei off to find Jamugha.
"Speak to Anda Jamugha,"
Temujin instructed his brothers, saying:
"The three Merkid chiefs have attacked me.
They've emptied my bed.
Don't you and I have the same ancestor?
Now how will we get our revenge on them?
They've taken part of my heart away.
Aren't we all from the same family?
Now how will we get satisfaction for what they've done?"
These were the words Temujin sent to his Anda Jamugha.
He also sent him the words that Toghoril Khan had spoken, saying:
"Keeping in mind that in the old days
your father, Yesugei the Brave, did me many favors,
I'll be your ally in this.
I'll start out from here with a force of twenty thousand men
forming the Right Hand of the army.
Tell Younger Brother Jamugha to start out with twenty thousand as well.
Let Younger Brother Jamugha decide when and where we should meet."
After the brothers repeated all this to Jamugha
he spoke to them, saying:
"When I hear Anda Temujin say,
'They've emptied my bed'
it brings pain to my heart.

36

When I hear him say,
'They've taken a part of my heart,'
it makes me grieve.
We'll get our revenge by destroying the clans of the Merkid,
and we'll save our Borte Ujin.
We'll shatter the clans of the Merkid
and get satisfaction for what they've done.
Together we'll bring back our Khatun Borte.
Toghtoga, who's frightened when he hears you strike a horse-blanket,
thinking it sounds like a war drum,
he must be camped now on the Steppe of Bugura.
Dayir Usun, who retreats as soon as you shake a quiver at him,
he must be at Talkhun Island, where the Orkhon and Selenge Rivers join.
Khagatai Darmala, who runs for the Black Forest as soon as he sees an uprooted weed blow across
          the steppe,
he must be camped on the Steppe of Kharaji now.
We'll go straight for the Kilgho River
where the riverweeds grow rich as a beard.
We'll lash the reeds into rafts
to carry our army across into the Merkid land.
As for the frightened Toghtoga,
we'll come down on him as if we leapt down through the smoke-hole of his tent,
beating down the tent-frame and leaving it flat.
We'll fight until his wives and his sons are all dead.
Striking his door-frame, where his guardian spirit lives,
we'll break it to pieces.
We'll fight till his people are completely destroyed,
until in their place there is nothing but emptiness."
Then Jamugha sent this message back with the brothers:
"Take these words to Anda Temujin and my Elder Brother Toghoril Khan.
Say that, as for me,
I've made sacred offerings to my standard
and held it up for all to see.
I've beaten my black bull-hide drum and made it sound like the thunder.
I've mounted my black warhorse.
I've put on my armor made hard as iron.
I've raised my steel lance.

I've placed on my bowstring a beautiful arrow edged with peach-bark.
I'll go off to fight with the Merkid.
Say to them, as for me,
I've made offerings to my standard that waves in the wind,
and held it high overhead for all men to see.
I've beaten my ox-hide drum and made it sound like a thousand men charging.
I've mounted my warhorse with the black stripe down its back.
I've laced up my breastplate of leather.
I've raised up my sword from its sheath.
I've placed on my bowstring an arrow I've marked with my enemy's name.
Let's all die together fighting the Merkid.
Have Elder Brother Toghoril Khan start out,
and when his forces have passed by Anda Temujin's camp,
below Mount Burkhan Khaldun,
we'll meet at Botoghan Bogorji at the head of the Onan River.
I've already gathered ten thousand soldiers,
and I'll assemble ten thousand more.
With twenty thousand soldiers we'll start up the Onan
and join the force of the Right Hand.
The place that we'll meet will be Botoghan Bogorji."
Khasar and Belgutei rode back to Temujin with Jamugha's reply.
Temujin then sent the message to Toghoril Khan.
Having heard Jamugha's reply
Toghoril Khan started out with his army.
Temujin said to his people:
"The Kereyid army is coming.
We will camp below Burgi cliff
in front of Mount Burkhan Khaldun."
Since his own people were camped there,
Temujin moved up the Tungelig and shifted his camp to the Tana Stream below Mount Burkhan
        Khaldun.
As Temujin moved out his people
Toghoril Khan, commanding ten thousand men,
and Jakha Gambu, Toghoril's younger brother, commanding ten thousand,
had nearly reached Burgi cliff.
The two camps moved together and united their forces.
Temujin, Toghoril Khan, and Jakha Gambu brought their forces to Botoghan Bogorji,

at the head of the Onan as they'd been instructed.
Jamugha was already there with his army
and had been waiting three days.
Jamugha stood at the head of his army of twenty thousand men
and Temujin, Toghoril Khan, and Jakha Gambu rode up at the head of their army.
As the leaders recognized each other
Jamugha spoke first, saying:
"Didn't we say to each other,
'Even if there's a blizzard,
even if there's a rainstorm,
we won't arrive late'?
Aren't the Mongol a people whose word is sacred?
Haven't we said to each other,
'Let's get rid of anyone who can't live up to his word'?"
Toghoril Khan answered Jamugha's criticism by saying:
"We've arrived three days late, you're correct.
Let Younger Brother Jamugha decide who he'll punish and who he'll blame."
Having settled this score
they moved their forces from Botoghan Bogorjin to the Kilgho River
where they built rafts to cross over to the Bugura Steppe,
into Toghtoga Beki's land.
They came down on him as if through the smoke-hole of his tent,
beating down the frame of his tent and leaving it flat,
capturing and killing his wives and his sons.
They struck at his door-frame where his guardian spirit lived
and broke it to pieces.
They completely destroyed all his people
until in their place there was nothing but emptiness.
But while Toghtoga Beki lay sleeping before the attack
fishermen, trappers, and hunters who lived by the Kilgho River came to warn him.
Running through the night
they brought news that the army was coming.
"Our enemies have thrown themselves across the river!" they cried.
And hearing this Toghtoga and Dayir Usun gathered a few followers,
with nothing but the clothes on their backs,
and escaped down the Selenge River to the Barghujin region.
As the Merkid people tried to flee from our army

running down the Selenge with what they could gather in the darkness,
as our soldiers rode out of the night capturing and killing the Merkid,
Temujin rode through the retreating camp shouting out:
"Borte! Borte!"
Borte Ujin was among the Merkid who ran in the darkness
and when she heard his voice,
when she recognized Temujin's voice,
Borte leaped from her cart.
Borte Ujin and Old Woman Khogaghchin saw Temujin charge through the crowd
and they ran to him,
finally seizing the reins of his horse.
All about them was moonlight.
As Temujin looked down to see who had stopped him
he recognized Borte Ujin.
In a moment he was down from his horse
and they were in each other's arms, embracing.
There and then Temujin sent off a messenger
to find Toghoril Khan and Anda Jamugha, saying:
"I've found what I came for.
Let's go no further and make our camp here."
When the Merkid who ran from us in the night saw our army had halted
they halted as well and spent the night where they'd stopped.
This is how Temujin found Borte Ujin,
saving her from the Merkid.

This attack had been brought on by the three Merkid chiefs,
Toghtoga Beki, Dayir Usun, and Khagatai Darmala.
They'd attacked Temujin with an army of three hundred men, saying:
"Long ago Yesugei the Brave stole Mother Hogelun
from our Younger Brother Chiledu."
So they attacked Temujin, Yesugei's son, to get their revenge.
They pursued Temujin,
chased him three times around Mount Burkhan Khaldun
and took Borte Ujin from his camp.
They gave her to Chilger the Athlete,
Chiledu's younger brother, as revenge.
She'd lived with Chilger since the day she was taken.

As our army came down on the Merkid
  Chilger the Athlete ran from us, saying:
"It may be the fate of a crow to eat nothing but scraps of dead flesh,
  but still he may think to himself,
 'Someday I'll eat goose and crane.'
  Now I've laid my hands on Borte Ujin
  and become a plague to my people for doing it.
  The evil Chilger has stretched out his neck,
  just waiting for someone to cut off his head.
  Now I'll have to run away in the darkness.
  How could I fight?
  After all that I've done who'd ever fight by my side?
  It may be the fate of the buzzard to eat rats and mice
  but still he may think to himself,
 'Someday I'll eat swan and crane.'
  Now I've taken the beautiful Ujin into my tent
  and become a plague to my people for doing it.
  I've stretched out my neck for someone to come and cut off my head.
  And now when my life is as worthless as sheep dung
  I'll have to escape into the dark hollows and canyons.
  Now when my life is as worthless as sheep dung,
  who'd throw up a fort to defend me?"
  and he ran from our army and escaped in the night.

Khagatai Darmala was captured and forced to wear a wood cangue.
  He was placed at the head of the army
  and told to lead them back to Mount Burkhan Khaldun.
  One of the soldiers told Belgutei:
"Your mother is also a captive here.
  She's somewhere in this camp."
  Belgutei set out to find his mother's tent
  but as he entered her tent by the right side, his mother—
  she was wearing only a poor sheepskin dress—
  went out by the left side to avoid him, saying:
"I've heard that my sons have become khans,
  while I've been a slave in the tent of a commoner.
  Now I can't look my sons in the face."

She ran from the camp and hid in the deepest part of the forest.
They searched everywhere for her
but she couldn't be found.
"Bring me my mother!" Belgutei Noyan cried,
and he shot every person of Merkid blood he could find with blunt arrows.
He assembled the three hundred Merkid,
the ones who'd attacked Temujin at Mount Burkhan Khaldun,
and he executed them all
along with the seed of their seed
so that they were extinguished like a fire
and their ashes blown away in the wind.
From their women who remained he took as his wives those fit to be wives.
From the rest he took as his slaves those fit to be slaves.

Temujin thanked Toghoril Khan and Jamugha for their help, saying:
"Because I was joined by my father the Khan and Anda Jamugha
my strength was increased by Heaven and Earth.
In the name of Eternal Blue Heaven
with the aid of Our Mother the Earth
we've torn out the hearts of the Merkid warriors,
we've emptied their beds and killed all their sons,
we've captured all the rest of their women.
Now that we've scattered the Merkid we should go back."

When the Merkid people ran from our army
our soldiers found a boy with a hat made from sables,
with fine doeskin boots
and clothes beautifully crafted from striped sable furs.
His name was Kuchu,
a five-year-old boy whose eyes contained fire.
He'd been left behind in the camp when the Merkid abandoned it
and our soldiers made a gift of him to Mother Hogelun.

So the forces of Temujin, Toghoril Kahn, and Jamugha,
who'd united to attack the Merkid clans,
who'd thrown open the Merkid's locked tents,
who'd reduced the Merkid's noblest women to slaves,

withdrew from Talkhun Island where the Orkhon joins the Selenge.
Temujin and Jamugha kept their forces together
riding back to the Khorkhonagh Valley to camp.
Toghoril Khan's army rode to the far side of Burkhan Khaldun
down the Hokortu Valley.
They rode on through Khachaguratu and Huliyatu Subchid
hunting as they went,
and finally returned to their camp
near the Black Forest on the Tula River.

The Wars in Mongolia

Temujin and Jamugha pitched their tents in the Khorkonagh Valley.
With their people united in one great camp,
the two leaders decided they should renew their friendship,
their pledge of anda.
They remembered when they'd first made that pledge,
and said, "We should love one another again."
That first time they'd met Temujin was eleven years old.
In those days
when he and his family had been abandoned by the Tayichigud,
he'd first met Jamugha,
a young noble of the Jadaran clan,
and they'd played at games of knucklebone dice on the banks of the Onan,
casting bones on the frozen waters of the Onan.
Jamugha had given Temujin the knucklebone of a roebuck
and in return Temujin gave Jamugha a knucklebone of brass.
With that exchange the two boys had pledged themselves anda forever.
Then later that spring
when the two were off in the forest together shooting arrows,
Jamugha took two pieces of calf-horn.
He bored holes in them,
glued them together to fashion a whistling arrowhead,
and he gave this arrow as a present to Temujin.
In return Temujin gave him a beautiful arrow with a cypresswood tip.
With that exchange of arrows
they declared themselves anda a second time.
So Temujin and Jamugha said to each other:
"We've heard the elders say,
'When two men become anda their lives become one.
One will never desert the other and will always defend him.'

44

This is the way we'll act from now on.
We'll renew our old pledge and love each other forever."
Temujin took the golden belt he'd received
in the spoils from Toghtoga's defeat
and placed it around Anda Jamugha's waist.
Then he led out the Merkid chief's warhorse,
a light yellow mare with black mane and tail,
and gave it to Anda Jamugha to ride.
Jamugha took the golden belt he'd received
in the spoils from Dayir Usun's defeat
and placed it around the waist of Anda Temujin.
Then he led out the whitish-tan warhorse of Dayir Usun
and had Anda Temujin ride on it.
Before the cliffs of Khuldaghar
in the Khorkhonagh Valley,
beneath the Great Branching Tree of the Mongol,
they pledged their friendship and promised to love one another.
They held a feast on the spot
and there was great celebration.
Temujin and Jamugha spent that night alone,
sharing one blanket to cover them both.

Temujin and Jamugha loved each other for one year,
and when half of the second year had passed
they agreed it was time to move camp.
It was the sixteenth day of the summer's first moon,
the Red Circle day,
when they broke their camp and set out.
They rode together at the head of the carts
as the camp moved across the steppe,
and Jamugha turned to his friend, saying:
"Anda, Anda Temujin,
let's pitch our camp near the mountains.
Let the cattle herders make a camp for themselves.
Let's pitch our camp near the stream.
Let the shepherds look for their own food."
Temujin couldn't understand what Jamugha's words meant.

45

He said nothing in reply
and brought his horse to a stop,
allowing the carts of the travelling camp to pass by
until he saw the carts of his own family's tents.
He rode up to the cart where Mother Hogelun was riding
and said to her:
"Anda Jamugha said to me,
'Let's pitch our camp near the mountains.
Let the cattle herders make a camp for themselves.
Let's pitch our camp near the stream.
Let the shepherds look for their own food.'
I did not understand what he meant so I said nothing.
I've come to you thinking,
'I'll ask my mother if she knows what he means.' "
Before Mother Hogelun could answer
Borte Ujin spoke up, saying:
"They say Anda Jamugha's a fickle man.
I think the time's come when he's finally grown tired of us.
These words are meant to cover some kind of plot.
When he stops, let's not pitch our camp.
Let's tell our people to keep right on moving,
and if we travel all night
by daybreak our camps will be well separated."

Agreeing with what Borte Ujin had said,
when Jamugha stopped to pitch camp
Temujin ordered his people to keep moving,
and they drove their carts on through the night.
As they travelled Temujin's people passed by the Tayichigud camp.
When the Tayichigud heard them approaching
they fled from their camp toward the place Jamugha had pitched his tents.
When Temujin's people reached the camp the Tayichigud had abandoned
they found a young boy named Kokochu who'd been left behind
and they gave him to Mother Hogelun.
From that time on
Mother Hogelun took care of him.

After travelling all that night
they halted at dawn to see who had followed them.
Camping circles from nearly all of the clans had chosen to follow Temujin.
People arrived from the Jalayir,
from the Onggur and the Manghud.
Ogele Cherbi, Bogorchu's kin, joined from the Arulad,
and Jelme's younger brother, Subetei the Brave,
left the Uriangkhai to join him.
People came in from the Besud, from the Suldus and the Khongkhotan.
Chaghagan Uua, chief of the Chinos clan,
came to join from Jamugha's camp.
Camp circles arrived from the Sukeken,
from the Olkhunugud, the Dhorolas, the Dorben,
from the Noyakin, the Oronar, and the Barulas.

Then in came Khorchi of the Bagarin.
When Khorchi arrived he spoke with Temujin, saying:
'My people are descended from the woman Holy Ancestor Bodonchar captured
and took for his wife.
Because of this, we're such close kin to Jamugha
that we're just like people who share the same mother's belly,
like people who come from the waters of the same mother's womb.
We'd never have left Jamugha's camp.
But a sign from Heaven came to me in a dream
and told me that Temujin was meant to be our leader.
In this dream I saw a great cow enter our camp.
First she circled Jamugha,
then she charged at his tent,
then charged at Jamugha himself,
striking him with her head and breaking one of her horns.
'Bring me my horn!' she cried to him,
'Bring me my horn!'
bellowing at him as she stood there
kicking up dustclouds with her hooves,
with one crooked horn on her head.
Then an ox with no horns at all

pulled up the tent stake and harnessed himself to the cart.
He drew away Jamugha's cart until he came up to Temujin.
He stopped there and began bellowing,
'Heaven and Earth have agreed
that Temujin should be Lord of the Nation.
I've come to bring you the Nation.'
These are the signs I've seen and the dreams I've received.
Now, if you, Temujin, become Lord of the Nation,
just as I have predicted,
how will you show me your gratitude and make me rejoice?"
Temujin answered him:
"If I am allowed to rule the Nation
I'll make you a captain of ten thousand men."
But Khorchi replied:
"What kind of happiness will being the captain of ten thousand men bring me?
Me, a man who's foretold great things to come!
After you've made me a captain of ten thousand men
allow me to choose thirty wives
from among the most beautiful girls you've assembled.
And remember everything I've said will come to pass."

Later Daritai, Temujin's uncle, arrived with a camp circle of followers,
along with people from the Geniges, Jadaran, and Saghayid clans.
When Temujin had moved his camp to Kimurgha Stream
Sacha Beki and Taichu, the eldest descendants of Khabul Khan,
left Jamugha and brought with them the Jurkin clan to join Temujin.
Then Khuchar Beki, son of Temujin's uncle Nekun Taisi, joined as well.
Finally Altan, the eldest descendant of Khutula Khan, arrived.
All these men left Jamugha to join Temujin's camp at Kimurgha Stream.

Then they moved the whole camp
to the shores of Blue Lake in the Gurelgu Mountains.
Altan, Khuchar, and Sacha Beki conferred with each other there,
and then said to Temujin:
"We want you to be khan.
Temujin, if you'll be our khan
we'll search through the spoils

for the beautiful women and virgins,
for the great palace tents,
for the young virgins and loveliest women,
for the finest geldings and mares.
We'll gather all these and bring them to you.
When we go off to hunt for wild game
we'll go out first to drive them together for you to kill.
We'll drive the wild animals of the steppe together
so that their bellies are touching.
We'll drive the wild game of the mountains together
so that they stand leg to leg.
If we disobey your command during battle
take away our possessions, our children, and wives.
Leave us behind in the dust,
cutting off our heads where we stand and letting them fall to the ground.
If we disobey your counsel in peacetime
take away our tents and our goods, our wives, and our children.
Leave us behind when you move,
abandoned in the desert without a protector."
Having given their word,
having taken this oath,
they proclaimed Temujin khan of the Mongol
and gave him the name Chingis Khan.

Once Chingis had been elected
Ogele Cherbi, Bogorchu's young kinsman,
was named as his archer.
Soyiketu Cherbi promised him:
"I'll see to it
you'll never miss your morning drink,
you'll never miss your evening meal,"
and he became head cook.
Degei promised him:
"I'll see to it
that a lamb is brought in for the morning broth,
that another's brought in for the evening.
I'll herd the speckled sheep

and see that your carts are filled with their wool.

I'll herd the yellow sheep

and see that your flocks are filled with their number,"

and he became head shepherd.

Then his younger brother, Guchugur, promised:

"I'll see to it

that the lynch-pins are always tight on the wheels of your carts,

that the axletree doesn't break when the carts are on the road.

I'll be in charge of the tent carts."

Dodai Cherbi promised:

"I'll be in charge of the men and women who serve in your tents."

Then Chingis appointed three men,

along with his brother Khasar,

to be his personal swordsmen, saying:

Anyone who thinks they are stronger,

you'll strike off their heads.

Anyone who thinks they're more courageous,

you'll cut them in two.

My brother Belgutei will bring the geldings in from the pasture.

He will be in charge of the horses.

Mulkhalkhu will be in charge of the cattle.

Arkhai Khasar, Taghai, Sukegei, and Chakhurkhan,

these four warriors will be like my arrows,

like the arrows I shoot near and far."

Then Subetai the Brave promised him:

"I'll be like a rat and gather up others,

I'll be like a black crow and gather great flocks.

Like the felt blanket that covers a horse,

I'll gather up soldiers to cover you.

Like the felt blanket that guards a tent from the wind,

I'll assemble great armies to shelter your tent."

Then Chingis Khan turned to Bogorchu and Jelme, and said:

"You two,

from the time when there was no one to fight beside me but my own shadow,

you were my shadow and gave my mind rest.

That will always be in my thoughts.

From the time when there was nothing to whip my horses with but their own tails,

you were their tails and gave my heart peace.
That will always be in my heart.
Since you were the first two who came to my side
you'll be chiefs over all the rest of the people."
Then Chingis Khan spoke to the people, saying:
"If Heaven and Earth grant me their protection so that my powers increase,
then each of you elders of the clans
who've chosen to leave Anda Jamugha and follow me
will be happy with the choice that you've made.
I'll give you each your position and office."

Chingis sent messengers to Toghoril Khan of the Kereyid, saying:
"They've made Temujin khan and given him the name Chingis Khan."
Toghoril Khan sent a message back saying:
"You're correct to make my son Temujin your khan.
How could the Mongol survive without a ruler?
Never go back on your decision.
Now that you've put this collar on your coat never remove it."
Then Chingis sent his warriors Arkhai Khasar and Chakhurkhan
off with a message to Jamugha,
and Jamugha sent a message back addressed to Altan and Khuchar, saying:
"You two,
why have you done this to us?
Why have you come between Anda Temujin and myself?
It's as if you came at us with a knife,
slashing our legs,
stabbing our sides to keep us apart.
Why didn't you elect Anda Temujin khan while we were still together?
What thoughts are behind this move to elect him now?
Altan and Khuchar,
don't forget these promises you've made.
See to it that my anda's mind is at rest and serve him well."

Sometime later, Taichar, a young kinsman of Jamugha's,
set out to steal the horses of our kinsman, Jochi Darmala.
Jochi Darmala's horses were grazing on the Donkey-back Steppe.
Taichar succeeded in stealing the entire herd

and drove them back to his camp near Mount Jalama.
None of Jochi Darmala's men had the courage to help him,
so he set out alone to find Taichar's camp and recover his herd.
He found Taichar's camp at night.
He concealed himself by grabbing his horse's mane
and lying low against its side,
so it looked like a riderless horse was wandering in off the steppe.
Hidden this way,
Jochi Darmala saw Taichar guarding the horses.
He shot Taichar in the back with an arrow,
killing him.
Then Jochi Darmala gathered his horses
and drove them back to his camp.
Because their kinsman, Taichar,
had been killed by one of our people,
Jamugha, as head of the Jadaran clan,
and thirteen other clans in his alliance,
raised an army of thirty thousand men
and rode through the Alagud and Turghagud Mountains to attack Chingis Khan.
Two men from the Ikires clan found Chingis in the Gurelgu Mountains
and warned him about the attack.
At that time our people numbered thirteen camping circles,
and Chingis Khan raised an army of thirty thousand men to fight Jamugha.
The two armies met at Seventy Marshes
and Jamugha forced Chingis Khan to retreat from there,
back to the Jerene Pass on the Onan.
Jamugha cried:
"We've forced them to hide from us in the Jerene Pass!"
When he came back to his camp
he ordered that the nobles of the Chinos clan
be boiled alive in seventy iron kettles.
Then he cut off the head of their chief, Chaghagan Uua,
tied it to the tail of his horse,
and dragged it behind him.

When Jamugha returned from the battle of Seventy Marshes
Jurchedei, leading the Urugud clan,

and Khuyildar, leading the Manghud,
both left his camp and joined Chingis Khan.
"Look at all the people who've left Jamugha to join us," said Chingis.
He conferred with Mother Hogelun and Khasar,
and together with Sacha Beki and Taichu of the Jurkin clan
they all agreed:
"Let's hold a feast on the banks of the Onan to celebrate their arrival."
At the feast the pitchers of kumis were served with great ceremony.
The first pitcher was poured for Chingis,
then Hogelun,
then Khasar,
then Sacha Beki and the others.
When one of our cooks named Shikigur began serving a pitcher,
he began pouring it first with Ebegei
who'd been only a minor wife to Sacha Beki's father.
Khorijin Khatun and Khugurchin Khatun,
the two Jurkin widows who ranked before her,
got up yelling:
"How can you start serving with Ebegei instead of us?"
and they struck down Shikigur where he stood.
Shikigur picked himself up and cried:
"Now that Yesugei the Brave and his elder brother Nekun Taisi are dead
look how the Jurkin think they can treat us!"
Belgutei had been given the job of watching our horses during the feast.
Buri the Athlete had been sent by the Jurkin to watch over theirs.
While the people were feasting
Belgutei caught a Khadagid man stealing a bridle from one of our horses.
Buri defended the man, who was his kinsman,
and began wrestling Belgutei.
As they fought, Buri tore the sleeve off of Belgutei's coat
and slashed the bare shoulder with his sword.
Chingis Khan, resting in the shade of a tree on the feasting grounds,
saw Belgutei walk away from his post
with a wound on his bare shoulder,
walking along as if nothing had happened
though the blood flowed from his wound.
Chingis ran to him, saying:

"How did this happen?
 Who did this to you?"
"It's not a bad wound," Belgutei answered,
"Don't start a fight among the people for me.
 I'm not badly hurt.
 It feels better already.
 These younger brothers have just joined their elder brothers
 and have hardly had time to get to know us.
 The elder brothers should be patient.
 Don't be too quick to strike back at them."
 Even with Belgutei trying to calm him
 Chingis Khan and his people tore branches off of the trees
 and gathered the wooden sticks from the milk buckets,
 and with these weapons they beat all the Jurkin,
 routing them and taking Khorijin and Khugurchin as hostages.
 After the fighting, the Jurkin offered to make peace
 and we agreed, returning the old women to them.

 Just then a messenger arrived, saying:
"When the Tatar chief, Megujin,
 disobeyed the commands of the Golden King of Cathay,
 the Golden King sent his general, Prince Hsiang,
 with an army against them.
 Prince Hsiang and his army are driving the Tatar
 up along the Ulja River.
 They are coming this way with all their herds and possessions."
 Chingis Khan spoke to the people, saying:
"The Tatar have been our enemies
 since the days when they killed our grandfathers and fathers.
 Now is our chance to attack them."
 He sent a messenger off to Toghoril Khan at once, saying:
"I've just heard that Prince Hsiang is marching
 up the Ulja River with a great army,
 driving the Tatar this way.
 Let's attack these Tatar together,
 since they're the ones who killed our grandfathers and fathers.
 Let my father Toghoril Khan send his troops quickly."

54

Toghoril Khan agreed, saying:
"My son, Temujin, speaks wisely.
We'll attack them together."
Three days later Toghoril Khan arrived at the Mongol camp
leading the Kereyid army.
Then Chingis and Toghoril
sent the same message to Sacha Beki and Taichu, saying:
"This is our chance to join together
to attack the people who killed our fathers and grandfathers."
They waited six days for an answer from the Jurkin
but when none came Chingis Khan and Toghoril Khan,
ordering their two armies to rise up and mount their horses together,
set out to attack the Tatar in the Ulja River valley.
They found them defending a fortress
built in the woods of birch and pine.
Chingis and Toghoril ordered their armies to attack,
and overrunning the Tatar defense,
they captured Megujin and killed him.
Chingis took the Tatar chief's silver cradle
and a blanket covered with pearls.
When Prince Hsiang found out
that Chingis Khan and Toghoril Khan had defeated the Tatar,
killing Megujin,
he was ecstatic.
As a reward he honored his new allies with Chinese titles.
To Chingis he gave the title Ja'ud Khuri, meaning Pacifier.
To Toghoril he gave the title Ong, meaning Prince.
So it's because Prince Hsiang gave Toghoril this name
that he was known from that time as Ong Khan.
Then Prince Hsiang spoke, saying:
"By joining us in the attack on the Tatar and killing Megujin
you've done a great service to the Golden King of Cathay.
I'll gladly report to him the service you've done.
Then we'll let him decide
whether Chingis Khan doesn't deserve an even greater title.
Maybe the King will decide to call you a Jautau, a Peacemaker."
Happy with his victory, Prince Hsiang withdrew to the south.

Chingis and Ong Khan then divided the spoils of the battle,
gathered their armies, and returned to their camps.

When our soldiers were gathering their spoils
from the Tatar fort in the pine woods,
they discovered a young boy who'd been left behind in the camp.
He had a gold ring in his nose,
and around his waist was a band of gold silk lined with sable.
Chingis Khan had this boy given to Mother Hogelun, saying:
"Here is a gift for you."
When Mother Hogelun saw him she said:
"He must be a nobleman's son.
His father must be from a good family."
She adopted him into her family,
calling him her sixth son.
She gave him the name Shigi Khutukhu and brought him up in her tent.

Chingis Khan had left the people who didn't go with the army
in a camp near Hariltu Lake.
The Jurkin attacked the camp,
stripping the clothes from fifty men and killing ten of us.
When those of us who'd stayed behind in the camp
told Chingis what the Jurkin had done
he grew furious, saying:
"How can they dare to do this to us?
When we held the feast together on the banks of the Onan
these same people beat the cook, Shikigur.
These same people stabbed Belgutei in the shoulder.
When they asked us to make peace
we returned the old women to them.
Then we sent them a message, saying:
'This is our chance to join together to attack the hated Tatar,
the people who killed our fathers and grandfathers.'
We waited six days for the Jurkin to answer and got no reply.
Having relied on our enemy they've become our enemy."
Chingis Khan set out to attack the Jurkin
and found them camped on the Kodoge Island in the Keluren.

His army routed them and took all they had.
Sacha Beki and Taichu tried to escape
with a few followers and the clothes on their backs
but they were captured at Teletu Pass
and brought before Chingis Kahn.
Chingis spoke to them, saying:
"What did you promise me long ago?"
And Sacha Beki and Taichu answered him:
"We have not kept our promise.
Make us honor our oath to you."
Remembering the oath that they'd sworn when they'd elected him khan,
they stretched out their necks to him.
And Chingis made them honor their oath,
executing them on the spot where they stood.

Having punished Sacha Beki and Taichu,
Chingis returned to the Jurkin camp.
As he was distributing the captives after the battle
the three sons of Telegetu the Rich stepped forward.
First the eldest, Gugun,
brought out his two sons, Mukhali and Bukha, saying:
"Let my sons be servants in your tent.
If they don't serve you well
cut off their feet.
Let them be the servants who open the door for you.
If they ever leave your service
you can kill them."
Then Chilagun brought his two sons, Tungge and Khashi, saying:
"Let my sons be the guards of your golden tent.
If they leave your golden tent
cut off their lives and leave them behind.
Let them open the wide door for you.
If they leave your wide door
cut out their hearts and leave them behind."
The youngest son of Telegetu, Jebke,
they gave to Khasar.

And Jebke brought a young boy named Boroghul from the Jurkin camp.
Presenting himself to Mother Hogelun
Jebke gave her the boy as a gift.
Mother Hogelun now had four boys to raise in her tent:
Guchu, who'd come from the camp of the Merkid,
Kokochu, who'd been found among the Tayichigud,
Shigi Khutukhu, who they'd found among the Tatar,
and Boroghul, who'd come from the Jurkin.
Mother Hogelun raised these four boys in her tent, saying:
"Thanks to these sons of mine
   my eyes will see everything in the daylight,
   my ears will hear everything in the night."

The Jurkin were descended from Khabul Khan's eldest son, Okin Barkhagh.
Since Okin was the eldest son,
Khabul Khan gave him the strongest men and the bravest fighters for his people,
men with great courage, great archers,
who fought with endurance and fury.
And since they had courage,
great skill with arrows, and fought with such fury,
they were soldiers that no one could beat.
They took the clan name of Jurkin, meaning the irresistible.
These are the people that Chingis Khan had just conquered.
And he disbanded the Jurkin,
making them his own private people.

One day Chingis said:
"Let's see Buri the Athlete and Belgutei wrestle."
When Buri the Athlete had been with the Jurkin
he'd lifted Belgutei with one of his hands during a wrestling match,
and grabbing Belgutei's legs out from under him,
threw him to the ground and pinned him there.
Buri the Athlete was the strongest man in the Nation.
When Chingis Khan asked to see Buri the Athlete and Belgutei wrestle
this time Buri, a man who could not be beaten,
let himself be thrown for a fall.

Still Belgutei wasn't strong enough to press Buri to the ground,
and instead took hold of his shoulders and sat Buri upright.
Then Belgutei looked over his shoulder to Chingis,
and as the two brothers' eyes met,
Chingis bit down on his lower lip.
Belgutei, seeing the signal,
pulled back on the two ends of Buri's collarbone
and brought down his knee as hard as he could onto Buri's back,
breaking his spine.
When he felt his back break, Buri the Athlete cried out:
"I could have defeated Belgutei,
but I was afraid I would anger the khan if I beat him.
I've let them trick me into taking a fall
and now they've killed me."
After Belgutei had broken his back
he dragged off the body of Buri the Athlete,
threw it out of the tent, and left.
Now of Khabul Khan's seven sons the eldest was Okin Barkhagh
and the next was Bartan the Brave.
Bartan's son was Yesugei the Brave, father of Chingis and Belgutei.
Khabul Khan's third son was Khutughtu
and his son was Buri the Athlete.
Instead of following the sons and grandsons of Bartan the Brave as he should have
Buri the Athlete left his lineage to follow the grandsons of Okin Barkhagh.
Because of this transgression,
Buri the Athlete, though he was the strongest man of the Nation,
was killed when Belgutei broke his back.

Then in the Year of the Cock
many clans joined together against us.
The Dorben made a peace with the Tatar to the east
and were joined by Buyirugh Khan of the Naiman from the west,
Khudukha Beki of the Oyirad from the forest to the north,
Khudu, Toghtoga Beki's son, from the Merkid,
and the Tayichigud led by Targhutai Kiriltugh and Aguchu the Brave.
All these people gathered at Alkhui Spring, saying:

"Let's elect Jamugha as our khan."
They performed the horse sacrifice,
cutting in two a stallion and mare,
and all swore an oath of allegiance together.
At an island in the Ergune River
where the Ken River pours in,
they elected Jamugha to lead them and gave him the title Gur Khan.
They agreed to attack Chingis Khan and Ong Khan together.
But before they could set out to attack
Khoridai rode off to warn Chingis Khan.
He found Chingis in the Gurelgu mountains.
When he told Chingis about the attack
Chingis sent word to Ong Khan.
Ong Khan gathered his army and rode quickly to Chingis's camp.
Once their armies had joined they said to each other:
"Let's go to war with Jamugha."
They rode down the Keluren River to meet the attack.
Chingis sent his cousins Altan and Khuchar
and his uncle Daritai in the lead,
and Ong Khan sent his son Senggum,
his brother Jakha Gambu,
and his commander Bilge Beki to join them.
They sent out sentries to watch from the Guiletu cliffs,
then others to watch from Mount Chegcher and Mount Chikhurkhu.
Just as the forward detachments were making their camp at Udkiya,
a sentry from Mount Chikhurkhu rode in saying:
"Jamugha's army's been seen."
So instead of pitching their camp
they rode off to meet the enemy soldiers to see who they were.
As the two groups approached our men shouted:
"Who are you?"
and they learned that they faced Aguchu the Brave from the Tayichigud,
the Naiman Buyirugh Khan,
the Merkid leader Khudu,
and the Oyirad Khudukha Beki.
These four men lead Jamugha's forces to battle.
But while they shouted questions back and forth it grew dark.

Agreeing that they would fight the next day
our soldiers rode back to where the main army waited.

At dawn the soldiers marched out to do battle at Koyiten.
Just as the two armies began to charge one another,
riding up and down the sides of the mountain,
reforming and charging in waves,
Buyirugh Khan and Khudukha, who were great shamans,
began to conjure a storm of darkness.
They began to raise winds and darkness in order to blind us,
when suddenly the storm turned.
Instead of striking our army their storm blinded their own men.
Their soldiers fell into ravines on the mountainside
unable to see, crying:
"Heaven's turned against us!"
and their army dispersed.
Buyirugh Khan left Jamugha and rode off for the Altai to the west.
Khudu retreated with his people north to the Selenge River.
Khudukha Beki ran back to the forests as far as the Shisgis.
And Aguchu the Brave led the Tayichigud back to the Onan.
Jamugha attacked and robbed the camps
of the very people who had elected him khan,
then took his own forces away down the Ergune.

Seeing all this,
Ong Khan went off in pursuit of Jamugha down the Ergune,
while Chingis Khan led his army after the Tayichigud forces.
When Aguchu the brave reached his camp on the Onan
he gathered all the Tayichigud.
His soldiers reformed their ranks for one last stand
and when Chingis arrived they rode out against him.
We fought the Tayichigud
and the killing was heavy on both sides until darkness fell.
When night finally came
the exhausted armies pitched their tents where they'd fought,
making their camps so close that they slept side by side.
Even the people in the Tayichigud camp who'd tried to escape

made their camp right there on the field with their soldiers.
During the fighting Chingis Khan was hit in the neck vein by an arrow,
and unable to stop the bleeding, he began to lose strength.
At sunset he had to make his bed where he'd fallen,
so close to the enemy that they slept side by side.
Jelme watched over him,
sucking and sucking the blood from his wound
until Jelme's mouth and chin were stained with Chingis's blood.
With no one to help Jelme watched over Chingis.
He did this till midnight,
sucking the wound clean again and again,
swallowing what blood he could,
spitting the rest out on the ground,
then at midnight Chingis Khan opened his eyes and said:
"My blood has dried up.
I am thirsty."
Jelme took off his hat, his boots and his clothing,
everything but his breechcloth,
and ran out in the darkness to the enemy camp,
the camp so close by that they slept side by side.
He searched through all the Tayichigud carts,
looking for mare's milk, but couldn't find any.
When the people had fled from us
they'd let loose their mares and so had no milk.
When he couldn't find mare's milk
he found a large covered bucket of curds,
and lifting the bucket onto his shoulders,
he ran back with it.
All this time no one had seen him;
he'd been protected by Heaven.
When he returned with this bucket of curds,
then he had to go off and find water.
Finding water,
he mixed up a drink with the curds for Chingis to drink.
The Khan drank three times from this mixture,
and felt his strength returning.
"The brightness comes back to my eyes," he said, sitting up.

As he sat up dawn was breaking
and the field was filling with sunlight.
He look around him
and saw the mire of blood where Jelme had spit the blood from his wound.
"What's this?" Chingis asked him,
"Why couldn't you spit the blood further away?"
Jelme answered:
"You were badly wounded
and I was afraid to leave your side for a second.
I swallowed as much blood as I could
and spit the rest on the ground.
You were bleeding many hours.
How much blood can a man swallow?"
Chingis Khan asked him:
"While I was lying there bleeding
why did you take off your clothes and run to the enemy camp?
If they captured you
would you have said I was wounded?"
And Jelme replied:
"I had a plan.
I took off my clothes so that if they captured me I'd say to them,
'I've decided to join you.
But when my own people realized I was deserting, they said,
"Let's kill him,"
and they stripped off my clothes as you see.
Before they could kill me I escaped and ran here to join you.'
Thinking I was telling the truth
they'd give me new clothes and a horse.
As soon as I got on the horse
I'd surprise them by riding right back.
All that would've taken no time at all,
and I'd've been back at your side.
So because I knew I had to find something to quench your thirst
in the blink of an eye I went off and came back to you."
And Chingis Khan said:
"Ah, Jelme,
long ago when the three Merkid chiefs

chased me three times around Mount Burkhan Khaldun,
that was the first time you saved my life.
Then sucking my wound with your mouth till the bleeding dried up,
you've given me back my life a second time.
Then when I was dying of thirst
you risked your life for me.
In the blink of an eye you ran into the enemy camp.
You returned with a drink for me and gave me my life back again.
I'll remember these three services you've performed for me."

At dawn we could see that the enemy soldiers
who'd slept side by side with us
had run off in the night.
The people who thought they'd be unable to escape
and so had camped there with their soldiers were still there.
Chingis Khan rose from where he'd spent the night
and as he gathered the people who had tried to escape
he heard a voice shouting: "Temujin!"
He saw a woman dressed in red crying to him from a nearby pass.
He sent a rider up to meet her, asking:
"Who's wife is calling me?"
She sent the rider back, saying:
"I'm Sorkhan Shira's daughter, Khadagan.
Your soldiers have captured my husband and are about to kill him.
'Temujin will save him,' I thought,
and I cried and shouted for you."
When Chingis Khan heard this he rode up the mountain,
and dismounting beside Khadagan, they embraced.
But our soldiers had already killed her husband by the time he arrived.

Chingis Khan gathered all the people back in the camp
and pitched his tents there for the night.
At the evening meal he had Khadagan sit beside him
and the following day Sorkhan Shira and Jebe,
both men who had served the leaders of the Tayichigud clan,
came to offer themselves to Chingis.
When Chingis saw Sorkhan Shira he said:

"You and your sons took the wood from my neck,
  took the cangue from my collar.
  Why have you taken so long to come join me?"
  Sorkhan Shira answered him:
"I often thought about the situation I was in
  and said to myself, 'Don't be too quick.
  If I go off to join Temujin the Tayichigud will kill all my family,
  make them blow away like the ashes of an abandoned fire.
  They'll take my wife and my sons, everything I leave behind.'
  So I was patient
  and now that the right moment's here we've come to join our khan."
  When he'd finished this speech Chingis Khan nodded and said:
"You've done the right thing."

  Then Chingis Khan spoke again, saying:
"Just as the two armies began to charge one another at Koyiten,
  riding up and down the sides of the mountain,
  reforming and charging in waves,
  someone shot an arrow at me from up on the ridge.
  Who was it who was able to fire an arrow from up on the mountain
  that pierced the spine of my white-mouthed warhorse?"
  Jebe answered him:
"I shot the arrow at you from up on the mountain.
  If you kill me right here
  I'll fertilize a bit of dirt the size of your hand.
  But if the Khan will allow me to live
  I'll ride out in his service and cut the deepest waters in two,
  split the brightest diamond.
  Just let him give me the order, 'Go here in my name,'
  and I'll be there with a force that will shatter blue rock.
  Just let him give me the order to attack
  and I'll charge with a force that will smash black stone to pieces."
  Chingis answered him:
"Usually a man who's fought against us is the last to admit it.
  He'll lie about what he's done or simply hide out of fear.
  But this man doesn't deny that he's fought us;
  in fact he declares it!

Here's a man who'll tell you straight what he's done
and here's a man that I'll have in my army.
They say his name is Jirghogadai
but I'll give him a new one.
Since he's the man who shot my warhorse in the spine,
the horse who'd been my finest weapon in war,
I'll name him Jebe, 'the weapon.'
From now on that is your name
and you'll ride by my side."
And this is how Jebe of the Tayichigud clan joined Chingis Khan.

Chingis then gathered his spoils from the Tayichigud camp
and executed the clan leaders,
their sons, and their grandsons,
so that their seed blew away in the wind like the ashes.
Then he moved his camp to Khuba Khaya for winter.

The Tayichigud leader Targhutai Kiriltugh had escaped into the forest,
but he was seized there by Old Man Shirgugetu,
one of his own servants,
and the Old Man's sons, Alagh and Nayaga.
Old Man Shirgugetu thought:
"Chingis Khan has good reason to hate Targhutai.
If I bring him to Chingis he'll be sure to reward me."
Targhutai was too fat to put on a horse
so they loaded him into a cart and rode off toward Chingis Khan's camp.
Targhutai's sons and brothers set off in pursuit
and when Old Man Shirgugetu saw their horses behind him
he jumped into the cart and sat on Targhutai's chest,
holding him down.
Then Old Man Shirgugetu pulled his knife and said to Targhutai:
"Your sons and your brothers are coming to take you.
I say to myself,
'I've laid hands on the man who's my rightful khan.'
If I don't kill you now
when they catch us they'll say,

'You've laid hands on him,' and they'll put me to death.
If I kill you now I'll die just the same.
So before I die I mean to take your life as my pillow."
Old Man Shirgugetu placed his knife against Targhutai's throat
and with all his strength Targhutai yelled to his sons and his brothers:
"Shirgugetu's about to kill me!
If he kills me what good will my corpse be to you?
Turn around before he cuts my throat.
Temujin won't kill me.
When Temujin was a boy I said,
'His eyes fill with fire,
his face fills with light.
With his father gone
he has no one in camp to show him what boys should know.'
So I said to myself,
'If I teach him things he looks like he'll learn.'
I taught him as if I were training a foal.
If I said,
'I should kill him,'
I could have killed him back then.
He knows that.
I hear that he's become filled with wisdom,
that his mind has opened with the years.
Temujin won't kill me.
But if you don't turn around quickly
Shirgugetu will have cut my throat!"
Targhutai's sons and brothers heard all this
and said to each other:
"We've come to save Targhutai's life.
If Shirgugetu kills him what good will his corpse be to us?
Let's turn around quickly,"
and they rode away.
So the Old Man and his two sons continued along
until they reached Khutukhul.
Here they stopped and Nayaga said:
"We've seized Targhutai and decided to take him to Chingis Khan.

When we get there Chingis will say to himself,
'These people have laid hands on their khan.
How can I trust them?
These aren't the kind of men I want in my camp.
People who rise up against their own khan should be killed.'
When we get there Chingis will have us executed for our troubles.
Instead we should let Targhutai go back by himself
and when we get to Chingis Khan's camp we'll say to him,
'We've come with nothing but the clothes on our backs
to offer our services to Chingis Khan.
We captured Targhutai Kiriltugh and were bringing him to you
but as we approached your camp we thought to ourselves,
"How can we do this to our own khan?
How can we watch him die before our very eyes?"
So we let him go.
Believing in your wisdom
we've come to offer our strength in your service.' "
His father and brother agreed with Nayaga's advice
so they set Targhutai free at Khudukhul
and went on to the camp without him.
When Old Man Shirgugetu, Alagh, and Nayaga arrived
Chingis Khan asked them:
"Why have you come?"
Old Man Shirgugetu answered:
"We captured Targhutai Kiriltugh and were bringing him to you,
but as we approached your camp we thought to ourselves,
'How can we let our khan die before our very eyes?'
So we let him go free and came here without him, saying,
'We'll offer our strength to serve Chingis Khan
and trust in his wisdom.' "
Hearing this Chingis said to him:
"If you'd come here bringing your own khan as a captive
I'd have had you all killed, you and your children.
That's what happens to people who lay hands on their khan.
So you made the right choice."
When Chingis learned that it had been Nayaga's advice that they'd followed
he favored the young man and made him a commander.

Later that year
when Chingis Khan made his camp at Tersud
Jakha Gambu of the Kereyid came to join him there.
When they were attacked by the Merkid
both joined forces and drove back the enemy.
After defeating the Merkid attack
Chingis Khan was joined by the ten thousand Tubegen people,
the Dongkhayid clans, and the other Kereyid people who'd dispersed.
And this is what had happened to Ong Khan at that time.
When Yesugei the Brave was alive
Ong Khan had lived in peace with the Mongol
and the two leaders had declared themselves anda.
This is why:
Ong Khan's father was Cyriacus Buyirugh Khan,
and after he passed away Ong Khan killed many of his younger brothers.
This caused his uncle Gur Khan to drive him away
and Ong Khan escaped with only a hundred soldiers at his side.
He came this way to Yesugei asking for help
and Yesugei gave Ong Khan the aid of his army.
Together they drove Gur Khan away toward the Tanghut
and Yesugei won back his people and throne for Ong Khan.
After this was accomplished they declared themselves anda.
Then later Ong Khan's younger brother Erke Khara
learned he too was to be killed by Ong Khan.
He escaped,
seeking aid and protection from Inancha Bilge Khan of the Naiman.
Inancha Bilge Khan sent his troops
and Ong Khan fled from the Naiman,
past three cities
to find shelter with the Khan of Black Cathay.
Ong Khan quarreled with this ruler as well and left his land,
travelling with his people past the cities of the Uighurs and Tanghuts.
By the time they reached Lake Gusegur
Ong Khan was living on the milk from five goats
and the blood he could prick from a camel.
When Chingis heard this had happened
he remembered that Ong Khan had been anda with his own father, Yesugei,

and he sent two messengers out from the Keluren River to find him.
Chingis told his people:
"Ong Khan has come to live with us.
He comes to us weary and hungry."
Chingis gathered taxes from his people to provide for Ong Khan,
and he brought him to live in his own camping circle.
When the winter came,
Chingis and Ong Khan rode together side by side,
and they set up their winter camp at Khuba Khaya.
But that winter Ong Khan's younger brothers
and many of their chiefs began to plot together against him.
They said:
"Our elder brother, the Khan, is a ruthless man with a terrible temper.
He's killed many members of his own family.
He's made himself subject to the Khan of Black Cathay.
He's made his own people suffer for these actions.
How should we deal with a man like this?
Back in his youth
he was captured by the Merkid at the age of seven.
They made him wear a coat of black-speckled goat fur
and pound grain in a mortar on the Bugura Steppe by the Selenge.
Cyriacus Khan saved him that time
only for him to be captured again by Ajai Khan of the Tatar,
this time when he was thirteen years old,
along with his mother.
The Tatar forced him to herd their camels
but he took one of their shepherds and escaped himself.
Then when the Naiman sent their army against him
he ran in fear to Black Cathay
all the way to the Chui River in the Moslem land.
Within a year he made trouble there too,
and we were travelling past the cities of the Uighur and Tanghut.
He was living on the milk from five goats
and the blood of a camel,
with nothing to ride but a blind yellow horse.
In this pitiful state
his son Temujin took him in and provided for him.

But despite all that Temujin's done for him
Ong Khan's still a ruthless and vile-tempered leader.
What will we do with him?"
But Altun Ashugh told Ong Khan before anything could be done.
Altun Ashugh went to him, saying:
"I was part of this plot.
But I can't bring myself to betray my own khan."
So Ong Khan arrested his younger brothers and their chiefs.
Jakha Gambu, afraid he'd be killed,
ran off and joined with the Naiman.
Ong Khan had the prisoners bound together and brought to his tent
where he addressed them, saying:
"When we were fleeing together through the lands of the Uighur and Tanghut
what did we say to each other then?
Even though you've all plotted against me
I can't bring myself to think as you do."
He spit in their faces
then ordered them set free.
After they'd seen what the khan had done to the conspirators
all the men in the tent arose and spit on them too.

At the end of that winter
in the autumn of the Year of the Dog,
Chingis Khan assembled his army at Seventy Felt Cloaks
to go to war with the four Tatar clans.
Before the battle began
Chingis Khan spoke with his soldiers and set down these rules:
"If we overcome their soldiers
no one will stop to gather their spoils.
When they're beaten and the fighting is over
then there'll be time for that.
We'll divide their possessions equally among us.
If we're forced to retreat by their charge
every man will ride back to the place where we started our attack.
Any man who doesn't return to his place for a counterattack will be killed."
Chingis Khan met the Tatar at Seventy Felt Cloaks
and made them retreat.

He surrounded them
and drove them back into their camp at Ulkhui Shilugeljid.
But as they destroyed the army of the four Tatar clans
Altan, Khuchar and Daritai ignored the orders Chingis had set down
and they stopped with their men to gather the spoils.
When Chingis Khan heard this, he said:
"They've broken their word,"
and he sent Jebe and Khubilai to punish them.
They took away from them everything they had gathered
and left them with nothing at all.
Having destroyed the Tatar army and taken their spoils,
a council was called to decide what to do with the captives.
Chingis Khan presided over the great council
in a tent set away from the rest of the camp.
They said to each other:
"Since the old days
the Tatar have fought our fathers and grandfathers.
Now to get our revenge for all the defeats,
to get satisfaction for the deaths of our grandfathers and fathers,
we'll kill every Tatar man taller than the linch-pin on the wheel of a cart.
We'll kill them until they're destroyed as a tribe.
The rest we'll make into slaves and disperse them among us."
That being what they decided to do,
they filed out of the tent.
As they came out the door of the council tent
the Tatar chief, Yeke Cheren, asked Belgutei:
"What have you decided?"
Belgutei told him:
"We've decided to kill every man taller than the linch-pin on the wheel of a cart."
Hearing that, Yeke Cheren warned all the Tatar survivors
and they threw up a fort to fight us off.
We had to storm this fort
and many of our soldiers were killed.
Then after we'd finally forced the Tatar to surrender their fort
and were measuring them against the height of a linch-pin and executing them,
they saw there was no way to escape death.
They said to each other:

"Every man place a knife in his sleeve.
  When the Mongol come to kill you,
  take that man as your pillow."
  And we lost many more of our soldiers.
  When all of the Tatar men taller than the height of a linch-pin were dead,
  Chingis Khan made this decree:
"Because Belgutei revealed the decision we'd reached in the great council
  many of our soldiers have died.
  From now on Belgutei won't be allowed to take part in such councils.
  He'll be in charge outside the council tent until it is over.
  Let him judge the fights in the camp
  and the men accused of lying and theft.
  After the council is over and we've all drunk the holy wine
  only then will Belgutei and Daritai be allowed to enter the tent."

  From among all the Tatar women
  Chingis Khan took Yeke Cheren's daughter, Yesugen Khatun,
  to be one of his wives.
  After she'd become Chingis Khan's wife she said to him:
"If the Khan loves me and wants to care for me,
  if he thinks I'm good enough to be his wife,
  then I have something to ask him.
  I have an older sister named Yesui
  who is a much better woman than I am
  and would make you a much better wife.
  But she was married to another man a short time ago
  and now since your attack on our camp
  who knows where she's gone?"
  Hearing this, Chingis Khan said to her:
"If your older sister is such a fine woman then I'll find her.
  And when I do will you give her your place?"
  And Yesugen Khatun answered him:
"If the Khan will search for Yesui,
  just for the pleasure of seeing her again
  I'd be happy to give her my place."
  Chingis ordered his soldiers to search for Yesugen's sister,
  and they found her travelling through the woods with her husband.

When the soldiers approached them he ran away,
and our men brought Yesui Khatun back to our camp.
When Yesugen Khatun saw her elder sister again
she remembered her promise.
She stood up and gave her place to her sister,
then sat down below her in the line of the wives.
This older sister was a beautiful woman
just as Yesugen had said,
and Chingis Khan loved her as well.
He married Yesui Khatun
and gave her a place in the line of his wives.

Having finished dividing the spoils,
one day Chingis Khan was resting outside his tent,
drinking together with his new wives,
Yesui Khatun and Yesugen Khatun.
As he sat there between the two sisters
he heard Yesui give a deep sigh.
Chingis became suspicious at this
and he called over his chiefs,
Bogorchu, Mukhali, and the others.
He ordered them:
"Have all the people in the camp line up by tribe.
Let no one stand next to a person who's not from his tribe."
When everyone had been lined up by tribe,
a fine-looking, elegant young man was left standing alone.
"Who are you?" they asked him, and he answered:
"I am the man Yeke Cheren gave his daughter in marriage.
I am Yesui's former husband.
When you defeated us I ran away in fear,
but then I said to myself,
'It's peaceful now.
How will they recognize me among so many people?'
So I came back to the camp."
When Chingis Khan heard what the fellow had said
he gave these orders to his men:
"This man was our enemy in battle and now he's come back.

74

What reason would he have to come back to our camp
except to spy on us?
What are you waiting for?
Get him out of my sight."
They took him away and cut off his head.

During that same Dog Year that Chingis Khan defeated the Tatar,
Ong Khan went to war with the Merkid.
He followed Toghtoga Beki all the way to the lowlands of Barghujin
and in the battle there Ong Khan killed the Merkid chief's eldest son,
captured his two daughters as well as his wives,
and took for himself Toghtoga's younger sons, Khudu and Chilagun,
as well as all of their possessions and people.
But Ong Khan offered none of his spoils to Chingis.

Then together Chingis Khan and Ong Khan
went to war with the Naiman led by Buyirugh Khan.
When they came on his forces at Ulugh Tagh,
Buyirugh Khan had no time to gather his army for a fight,
so he retreated back through a pass in the Altai mountains.
Chingis and Ong Khan followed him through the Altai,
riding down the Urunggu River valley.
Yedi Tublugh, a Naiman chief, hung back to spy on us,
but when he tried to escape our men by riding over the mountain
his saddle-strap broke and we captured him.
So without warning,
Chingis Khan and Ong Khan overtook the Naiman at Lake Kishil Bashi
and they destroyed Buyirugh Khan's army.
On their way back through the mountains
Chingis and Ong Khan were met by the great Naiman warrior Kogsegu Sabragh,
who'd assembled an army to fight them
at the mouth of the Bayidaragh Valley.
Chingis and Ong Khan assembled their armies,
but as it was already evening they agreed to fight the next day.
That night Ong Khan ordered his soldiers to light fires where they'd halted,
then he moved out his army up the Khara Segul under cover of darkness.
Jamugha rode off with Ong Khan that night

and Jamugha said to Ong Khan as they rode:
"My anda, Temujin, must secretly be sending messages to the Naiman.
He's no longer behind us.
My Khan, my Khan,
I am the sparrow who's always with you.
Anda Temujin is the lark who flies south when it's cold
and north when it's warm.
He's deserted you to join with the Naiman.
He's stayed behind to become a subject of the Naiman Khan."
Hearing what Jamugha was saying,
Gurin the Brave said to him:
"You know how to flatter at another's expense.
How can you say such things?
How can you slander and lie about your own brother,
a man who's done nothing wrong?"
Chingis Khan spent the night where he'd halted, still thinking:
"Tomorrow we'll fight,"
but at dawn he looked to where Ong Khan's army had been
and saw they were gone.
He said:
"They treat us like we were burnt meat left from a sacrifice,"
and he ordered his army to ride out the Eter Valley,
over the Altai,
pitching his camp finally back on the Donkey-back Steppe.
Chingis and Khasar didn't consider the Naiman worth fighting again.
But Kogsegu Sabragh attacked Ong Khan's forces from the rear
and routed them.
The Naiman fell on them at the Telegetu Pass
and captured the wives and sons of Ong Khan's son, Senggum,
and took away half of his people,
his herds, and provisions.
During the battle the Merkid princes, Khudu and Chilagun,
escaped from Ong Khan with their people
and rode back up the Selenge to rejoin their father, Toghtoga Beki.
After Kogsegu Sabragh had taken his spoils
Ong Khan sent a messenger to find Chingis Khan, saying:

"The Naiman have taken my people away,
  my wives and my sons.
  I ask that my son send me his four greatest heroes.
  Let them save my people for me."
Chingis responded by assembling his army
  and sending his four heroes,
  Bogorchu, Mukhali, Boroghul, and Chilagun,
  to fight for Ong Kahn.
Before the Mongol arrived
  Senggum had ordered his soldiers to fight the Naiman at Hulagan Khud.
As the Kereyid army started to charge
  Senggum's horse was killed by an arrow.
The Naiman were about to capture Senggum
  when the four Mongol heroes saved him.
They recaptured the Kereyid people,
  Ong Khan's wives and his sons,
  and drove off the Naiman.
Ong Khan said to them:
"Long ago when my people were taken
  they were returned to me by Temujin's father.
  Now my son, Temujin,
  has sent his four heroes and they've saved my people for me again.
  Let Heaven and Earth grant me protection
  for the way I will thank him for this act on his part."
Then Ong Khan spoke again, saying:
"When my people had completely deserted me,
  my anda, Yesugei the Brave, saved them for me.
  When they left me again,
  his son, Temujin, brought them back.
  This father and son have gathered the people who've left me,
  they've suffered and struggled to help me time and again.
  Now I'm growing old.
  Soon I'll be so old my body will go up into the mountains.
  When I'm so old that my corpse is placed on the cliffs
  who will rule over my people?
  My younger brothers are worthless men.

My only son, Senggum, is like having no son at all.
I'll adopt Temujin, making him Senggum's elder brother.
Then with two sons I'll be happy."

So before all his people in the Black Forest on the Tula,
Ong Khan and Chingis Khan declared themselves father and son.
They declared themselves father and son
because in the old days Chingis' father, Yesugei,
declared himself anda with Ong Khan,
and Chingis considered Ong Khan to be like his father,
and that's why now they said they were like father and son.
They promised each other:
"When we charge at the enemy in war
we'll charge out together.
When we go off to hunt the wild game
we'll hunt in one place.
If others envy our friendship
if some snake with sharp teeth tries to provoke us to fight,
we won't even listen to what he has to say.
Let's only listen to words we hear from the other man's mouth.
If some snake with long fangs tries to break up our friendship with slander,
we won't even listen to his lies.
Let's only believe what we know has come from the other man's tongue."
Pledging their word to each other,
they promised their friendship forever.
Then Chingis Khan thought to himself:
"Even though we are friendly,
let's be doubly friendly."
He asked that his eldest son, Jochi,
be given Senggum's sister, Chagur Beki, in marriage.
When he asked for her, he said:
"In exchange we'll give you Khojin Beki,
to marry Tusakha, Senggum's son."
But Senggum imagined he was someone too important for this.
He said:
"If one of our women would marry a Mongol
they'd make her sit at the servant's place
and stare at the back of the tent.

If one of their women would marry a Kereyid
we'd have her sit at the lady's seat
and face toward the door."
He thought he was too important.
He hated us and wouldn't agree to the marriages.

When Chingis Khan heard what Senggum had answered him,
in his heart Chingis knew
he'd lost all his feelings of friendship for Ong Khan and Nilkha Senggum.
Jamugha could tell that Chingis felt this way.
In the spring of the Year of the Pig,
Jamugha joined with Altan and Khuchar,
and along with the chiefs of three other clans
they plotted with Nilkha Senggum.
They gathered together on the Desert of Weariness beyond Mount Jejeger.
Jamugha slandered Chingis Khan, saying:
"Anda Temujin is sending messages back and forth to Tayang Khan of the Naiman.
While his mouth is saying words like 'father' and 'son'
his actions speak otherwise.
How can you trust such a man?
If you don't stop him now who will save you?
If you attack Anda Temujin now
I'll pledge to attack him from the rear."
Then Altan and Khuchar, Chingis Khan's cousins, said:
"We'll be happy to kill all the sons of Mother Hogelun
from the eldest to the youngest."
The chiefs of the other three clans added:
"We'll bind up his hands.
We'll tie up his feet.
But the best thing to do would be to take away all of Temujin's people.
If we take all his people
then what can he do to us?
If this is what Nilkha Senggum wants us to do
we'll follow him to the ends of the earth
or the bottom of the sea."

Nilkha Senggum sent a messenger to his father, Ong Khan,
to tell him the plan.

When Ong Khan heard what they'd said, he replied:
"How can you think such things about my son, Temujin?
In our times of greatest trouble he's been our support.
Now if we think badly of him
we're sure to lose Heaven's protection.
Jamugha doesn't know what he's talking about.
How do you know that he's telling the truth?"
Ong Khan wouldn't even consider the messenger's words
and sent him right back to Nilkha Senggum.
Senggum sent the messenger back again to his father, saying:
"The man has a mouth and a tongue.
Why shouldn't I believe what Jamugha says?"
But Ong Khan wouldn't even listen to what the messenger said.
Senggum was so upset by this
he went to his father himself this time, saying:
"Even now, when you're still alive,
Temujin has no respect for you.
So, my father the Khan,
when you're so old you choke on white milk,
so feeble you gag on black meat,
will Temujin allow us to rule our own people,
all these people your father, Cyriacus Khan, amassed?
Who'll rule the Kereyid people then?"
Ong Khan replied:
"How can I betray my own son?
How can we think evil of a man
who's supported us in our greatest troubles?
If we do we're sure to lose Heaven's protection."
Hearing this Nilkha Senggum grew so angry
he threw aside the door of the tent and stalked out.
And Ong Khan,
afraid Senggum would hate him if he didn't agree,
called him back, saying:
"If we do this
there's no way to know what Heaven will do to us.
How do you plan to kill my son, Temujin?
Do whatever you think you can do.

80

But know what you're doing."
So Senggum told Ong Khan what they had planned:
"He asked us to let his son marry our Chagur Beki.
Now we'll say to him,
'Come to our camp for the engagement feast.'
We'll set a day for the marriage and invite them to come,
and when he arrives we'll capture him."

Ong Khan agreed, and he sent a message to Chingis Khan saying:
"We'll give you Chagur Beki to marry your son.
Come to our camp for the engagement feast."
When he heard this
Chingis Khan gathered ten of his men to ride with him
and on their way they all spent the night in the tent of Father Munglig.
Father Munglig said to them:
"When you asked them for Chagur Beki before
these same people insulted us and wouldn't agree to the marriage.
Now, all of a sudden,
why have they invited you to a marriage feast?
Why all of a sudden should people who think that they're better than we are say to us,
'We'll give you our daughter'?
Are they being honest?
Are they telling the truth?
My son, it's you that they're after.
Make an excuse and send two of your men in your place.
Tell them,
'It's spring.
Our horses are thin.
We need time to fatten them up.' "
Chingis Khan sent two of his men in his place,
telling them:
"You go and eat the marriage feast."
When he left Father Munglig's tent
Chingis rode back to his own camp.

Senggum and the others saw the two Mongol arrive without Chingis Khan
and they said to themselves:

"He's felt a plot against him.
   We'll have to surround his tent
   and capture him tomorrow at dawn."
   Altan's younger brother, Yeke Cheren, went back to his tent
   and he spoke to his family about what they'd decided to do, saying:
"We said to each other,
 'Let's surround Temujin's tent
   and capture him early tomorrow.'
   If someone rode off to Temujin now and told him about this
   that messenger would get quite a reward."
   As he said this his wife, Alagh Yid, answered him:
"Why do you even say such a thing!
   What if someone heard you and did just that?"
   And as they said this to one another
   Badai, one of their herdsmen,
   came into the tent with some milk
   and overheard what they'd said.
   He went back to the cattle
   and told his friend Kishiligh, the herdsman, what Yeke Cheren had said.
   Kishiligh said to him:
"Let's go back there and see if it's true."
   He walked back to the tent where he saw Yeke Cheren's son, Narin Kegen,
   sitting outside whittling and polishing his arrows,
   and Narin Kegen was saying to himself:
"Why'd we talk so loud to each other before?
   We should've kept our mouths shut.
   If anyone heard us
   there'll be no one to keep them from talking."
   Then when he saw the herdsman nearby
   he said to Kishiligh:
"Go out to the pasture and bring me the White Merkid gelding
   and the Bay gelding with the black mane and tail.
   Harness them up.
   We're setting out early tonight."
   When Kishiligh came back to Badai, he said:
"I checked out what you've heard and it's true.
   The two of us should ride off with this news to Temujin."

They swore they'd help each other
and went out to the pasture to harness the White Merkid gelding
and the Bay gelding with the black mane and tail.
They took a lamb back to their tent
and secretly slaughtered it.
Then they boiled it,
using a fire they built from the wood in their beds.
They mounted their two horses under cover of darkness,
and rode through the night to Chingis Khan's tent.
When Badai and Kishiligh arrived at the Mongol camp it was night
and they stood to the north of the tent walls.
They repeated the words they'd heard Yeke Cheren speak,
and the things that his son, Narin Kegen, had said while polishing his arrows:
"Bring me the two geldings.
We set out early tonight."
Then Badai and Kishiligh said to him through the tent walls:
"If Chingis Khan will listen to us
we swear it's all true.
They all pledged their word and said,
'Let's surround Temujin and capture him.' "

When he heard what Badai and Kishiligh had to tell him
Chingis Khan sent word to all the men he could trust camped nearby.
They joined together.
Leaving behind anything that would slow them down,
they rode off in the night to the east.
He rode off to the far side of Mount Mau,
leaving Jelme guarding the rear.
They continued to ride
and by noon the next day they'd reached the Sands of Khalakhaljid
where they stopped to rest and to eat.
But even as they halted
two men who were guarding Alchidai's horses
saw the dust of the enemy army close behind,
to the other side of Mount Mau passing by the Red Willows.
These herdsmen rode back into the camp, crying:
"We've seen the enemy!"

driving their geldings before them.
They saw the dust rising on the other side of Mount Mau,
passing by the Red Willows, and they said:
"Ong Khan's army is coming behind us."
When Chingis Khan saw the dust rising
he ordered everyone to bring their geldings in from pasture.
They saddled their horses and set off to meet the enemy army.
If they had not seen them approaching
they would not have been ready to fight.

As the two armies approached
Jamugha was riding with Ong Khan.
Ong Khan turned to Jamugha and asked him:
"Of the people who ride with my son, Temujin,
who will fight us?"
Jamugha answered him:
"The Urugud and the Manghud clans are still with him.
Those people will fight us.
When they turn to attack they never break ranks.
When they turn to attack they hold their formation.
They're people who've used swords and lances since childhood.
They have black and speckled standards they carry to battle.
They're the ones we should be careful of in the fighting."
Ong Khan listened to this and said:
"If that's the case we'll have the brave men of the Jirgin,
led by Khadagh the Brave,
charge at them first.
Behind those
we'll have Achigh Shirun lead the ten thousand Tubegen.
They will be the second charge.
Behind the Tubegen forces
we'll have the brave men of the Dongkhayid clan.
And following the Dongkhayid
Khori Shilemun Taisi will lead out my thousand best dayguard to fight.
Behind the charge of the dayguard
the great middle army will follow."
Then Ong Khan spoke again, saying:

"Younger Brother Jamugha,
  you be in charge of the army."
  Hearing this Jamugha withdrew by himself,
  then speaking to a few close companions he said:
"Ong Khan has asked me to be in charge of his army.
  I've never been able to lead a successful charge against my own anda.
  Yet he goes ahead and asks me to lead the whole army.
  I think Ong Khan is even farther from being able to do this than I am.
  As an ally Ong Khan's limits are plain to see.
  I'll send word to my anda and warn him."
  In secret Jamugha sent a message to Chingis Khan, saying:
"Ong Khan has been questioning me.
  He asked,
  'Who will fight beside my son, Temujin?'
  and I told him the Urugud and the Manghud would be the first to attack us.
  Because of what I said
  he put the Jirgin first in the line of attack.
  Then Achigh Shirun will lead the ten thousand Tubegen,
  and behind the Tubegen will be the Dongkhayid.
  Then Khori Shilemun Taisi will lead out Ong Khan's own dayguard.
  Then Ong Khan said,
  'Behind these I will lead out the great middle army.'
  But when Ong Khan spoke again he appointed me, saying,
  'Younger Brother Jamugha,
  you be in charge of the army.'
  As an ally his limits are plain.
  He can't even set his own army in order.
  I've never been able to fight a battle with my anda.
  Ong Khan is even less able than I am.
  My anda, don't be afraid, but be careful."
  When Chingis Khan received this message
  he turned to Jurchedei of the Urugud clan and said:
"What do you say, Uncle Jurchedei.
  I'll have you lead the first charge."
  But before Jurchedei could even answer,
  Khuyildar the Wise of the Manghud clan spoke, saying:
"I'll fight for my anda and lead the first charge.

Just let my anda be sure that when I'm gone
there's someone to care for my orphans."
And Jurchedei answered:
"The Urugud and the Manghud will lead the charge for Chingis Khan."
Just as Jurchedei and Khuyildar assembled their soldiers
the Jirgin began their first attack.
As they rode out the Urugud and Manghud charged out against them
and drove back the attackers.
But as they drove back the Jirgin,
Achigh Shirun led the ten thousand Tubegen against them.
As the Tubegen charged into the battle,
Achigh Shirun struck Khuyildar and made him fall from his horse.
The Manghud withdrew to protect the wounded Khuyildar
but Jurchedei led his Urugud against the ten thousand Tubegen.
As he was driving the Tubegen charge back,
making them retreat,
the Dongkhayid forces charged into the battle.
But Jurchedei defeated the Dongkhayid charge.
As he drove back the Dongkhayid,
Khori Shilemun Taisi charged out with Ong Khan's thousand dayguard.
And Jurchedei was able to drive back this charge as well.
As Jurchedei forced the dayguard to retreat,
Senggum gathered up soldiers,
and without telling Ong Khan what he planned,
he led a charge against the Mongol.
As he charged at Jurchedei
he was struck in the cheek by an arrow and knocked from his horse.
When Senggum fell
the Kereyid army withdrew to guard him.

So after defeating the Kereyid in the battle,
just as the setting sun was touching the line of the hills,
our men returned to our camp carrying the wounded Khuyildar.
Chingis Khan gathered his army
and rode away from Ong Khan's forces,
and once they had put distance between them
they stopped for the night.

86

As they stood waiting for day to dawn they called roll.
They found that Chingis Khan's third son, Ogodei,
and his two heroes, Boroghul and Bogorchu, were still missing.
Chingis Khan spoke, saying:
"My faithful Bogorchu and Boroghul must have stayed behind with Ogodei.
Dead or alive, they would stay by one another."
We put our geldings out to pasture to graze for the night,
and Chingis Khan said:
"If they come after us from behind
we must be ready to fight them again,"
and he ordered his soldiers to be ready for another attack.
As they waited for daylight to come
they saw a single man riding up from the rear.
As he drew closer they saw it was Bogorchu.
As Bogorchu rode in,
Chingis Khan struck his breast and gave thanks to Eternal Heaven.
And Bogorchu said:
"As I charged at the enemy
my horse was struck down by arrows
and I was forced to run off on foot.
When the Kereyid stopped to guard over Senggum
I saw a pack-horse standing idle
whose pack had fallen off to one side.
I cut off the pack with my knife
and getting up on the horse,
I rode off to find your tracks.
When I finally found which direction you'd gone off,
I followed your trail until I found you."
Then a moment later they saw another man riding in.
As he rode closer they could see
two legs hanging down from his horse.
Though it had looked like only one man
when he rode in it was Boroghul riding double behind Ogodei,
and blood was flowing from the corners of Boroghul's mouth.
Ogodei had been wounded in the neck vein by an arrow,
and Boroghul had kept the wound open and clean by sucking it,
until the blood began to flow out the corners of his mouth.

When Chingis Khan saw what had happened to his son,
tears came to his eyes and there was pain in his heart.
He ordered someone to build a quick fire
and apply heat to the wound,
then he had another man bring Ogodei something to drink.
"If the enemy follows us, we'll attack them," he said.
Boroghul said:
"The dust of the enemy,
by the front of Mount Mau,
over toward the Red Willows,
their dust rises up in a long cloud and is moving away."
When he heard what Boroghul reported, Chingis Khan said:
"If they had followed us we would have fought them.
But if they ride away from us
then we'll reform our army and fight another time."
He gathered his forces and rode eastward up the Ulkhui Shilugeljid,
entering Dalan Nemurges.
Khadagan Daldurkhan came riding into our camp from behind.
He'd left his wife and his son with the Kereyid
and come to join Chingis Khan.
He brought news of Ong Khan, saying:
"When Ong Khan heard that his son, Senggum,
had been shot by an arrow, he said,
'We should have known better than to stir up Temujin's anger.
We should have known better than to provoke him to war.
Now we've brought this punishment on ourselves.
We've caused one of them to drive a nail through my son's cheek.
We must charge out against them to save the life of my son!'
But Achigh Shirun, who led the Tubegen,
stopped Ong Khan, saying,
'My Khan, my Khan, don't attack them now!
We prayed for a son to be born to you year after year,
offering prayers and sacrifices to Heaven,
crying to Heaven until Senggum was born.
Let's protect the life of the son that you have.
Most of the Mongol are already with us,
led by Jamugha, Altan, and Khuchar.

As for the ones who've gone off with Temujin,
where can they go now?
They've nothing to ride but a few horses,
nothing over their heads but the branches of trees.
If they don't come back to submit to us on their own accord
we can go out and round them up later,
gather them up in our skirts like dried horse-dung on the steppe.'
And Ong Khan said to him,
'Yes, my son must be tired and weak.
Take care of my son.
Carry him gently back to our tents.'
And he ordered his army to withdraw to the west."

Chingis Khan moved his people away from Dalan Nemurges,
up the Khalkha River,
then he stopped to count the men he had left.
When they counted they found there were two thousand six hundred soldiers.
Half of these rode along the west bank of the river with Chingis
and the other half,
the Urugud and Manghud clans,
rode along the eastern side.
They rode along the Khalkha River,
hunting to supply their food,
and Khuyildar led the forces on the east bank.
Though Chingis Khan had warned him not to hunt till his wounds had healed,
Khuyildar charged the game along the river.
As he charged his wounds reopened and he died.
Chingis Khan saw to it that Khuyildar's bones
were placed on Keltegei Cliff by Mount Nugu.
He knew that where the Khalkha emptied into Lake Buyur
the Ungirad chiefs made their camps.
So he sent Jurchedei with the Urugud soldiers on ahead, saying:
"If they say to you,
'Since the old days
the Ungirad people have thrived not on our strength in war
but on the loveliness of our daughters,
the beauty of our granddaughters,

then they'll surrender to you.
If they say to you,
'We'll fight,'
then we'll attack them."
When Jurchedei arrived the Ungirad chiefs surrendered
and Chingis Khan didn't harm them at all.

After the Ungirad surrendered
Chingis moved his camp east of the Tungge Stream.
From here he sent Arkhai Khasar and Sugegei Jegun off as messengers,
saying: "Go to my father the Khan and tell him,
'We've made our camp east of the Tungge Stream
where the pasture is good.
Our geldings are regaining their strength.'
Then say to him, 'My father the Khan,
what have I done to you that caused you to scare me this way?
And if you felt you had reason to punish me,
then why did you have to destroy the peace of my people
who are also your own sons and daughters?
You made them run from their homes,
scattering the smoke that rose up from their tents;
why did you have to scare them as well?
My father the Khan,
has someone come with a knife and stabbed at your side?
Has someone stood between us and provoked you to do this?
My father the Khan,
what did we promise each other on the banks of the Tula?
In the Red Hills by Mount Jorkhal what did we say?
Didn't we say,
"If some snake with sharp teeth tries to provoke us to fight
we won't even listen to what he has to say.
Let's only listen to words we hear from the other man's mouth"?
Did you bother to find out what I actually said before attacking me?
Didn't we say,
"If some snake with long fangs tries to break up our friendship with slander
we won't even listen to his lies.
Let's only believe what we know has come from the other man's tongue"?

Did you bother to speak to me face to face before becoming my enemy?
My father the Khan,
though my people are few we haven't made you search for a larger tribe.
Though I may not have been a perfect son
I haven't given you cause to search for anyone better.
If a cart with two axles breaks one the oxen can't pull it.
Am I not like your second axle?
If a cart with two wheels loses one it can no longer move.
Am I not like your second wheel?
If we speak of the old days
I recall that after your father, Cyriacus Buyirugh Khan, passed away
you became khan, saying,
"I am the eldest brother of his forty sons."
You had two younger brothers executed
and when your brother Erke Khara was also going to be killed
he escaped and surrendered himself to Inancha Bilge Khan of the Naiman.
When they told your uncle you had murdered your brothers
he attacked you and forced you to flee with only a hundred followers,
down the Selenge to Kharagun Pass.
Then you came to my father, Yesugei the Brave, and said to him,
"Save my people for me from my uncle, Gur Khan."
My father, Yesugei, said, "I'll save your people for you,"
and his army drove Gur Khan away toward the Tanghuts.
Then in the Black Forest of the Tula River
you pledged yourself anda with my father, Yesugei,
and thanking him you said,
"In thanks for what you've done
I'll return your help to the seed of your seed.
May the Heaven above and the Earth below
continue to protect me because of my gratitude."
Then when Erke Khara and Inancha Khan of the Naiman attacked you
you deserted your own people.
With a few followers you went to find shelter with the Khan of Black Cathay,
by the Chui River in the land of the Moslems.
Before a year had gone by you'd quarreled with that ruler too,
and travelling through the lands of the Uighurs and Tanghuts,
living on the milk from five goats

and the blood you could prick from a camel,
you came back riding a blind yellow horse.
When I heard that my father the Khan was in such a condition
I remembered the fact that you had declared yourself anda with my father
and I sent messengers to meet you,
then came back to meet you myself at Lake Gusegur.
I gathered taxes from my people and gave them to you,
remembering that you were my father's anda.
Isn't this why we declared ourselves father and son in the Black Forest by the Tula?
I took you into my camp circle and cared for you that winter
and in the fall when we attacked Toghtoga Beki and defeated him
I took all their herds, their grain, and their palace tents
and presented them to my father the Khan.
There wasn't a day I allowed you to go hungry.
There wasn't a month you weren't given the things that you needed.
Then we went to war against Buyirugh Khan of the Naiman
and followed him over the Altai,
from Ulugh Tagh down the Urunggu River Valley,
destroying his forces at Lake Kishil Bashi.
As we returned we met with Kogsegu Sabragh,
who'd gathered an army of Naiman to fight us in the Bayidaragh Valley.
Since it was already evening
we agreed to spend the night there, saying,
"We'll fight in the morning."
Then you, my father the Khan,
lit fires at your battle stations
and moved your army away up the Khara Segul under cover of darkness.
Early the next morning I saw you had left,
and saying "They treat us like we were burnt meat left from a sacrifice,"
I took my people out the Eter Valley,
over the Altai to the Donkey-back Steppe.
And Kogsegu Sabragh came after you
and took the wives and sons of Senggum,
took half of the people,
the herds, and the provisions of my father the Khan.
And Toghtoga Beki's two sons escaped from you,
and took all their people back to rejoin their father at Barghujin.

Then you, my father the Khan, said to me,
"Kogsegu Sabragh has taken my people.
My son, send me your four heroes."
I didn't act the way you had acted toward me.
I sent you my soldiers, led by my four heroes,
Bogorchu, Mukhali, Boroghul, and Chilagun the Brave.
Senggum's horse had been killed by an arrow
and the Naiman were about to take him when my four heroes arrived.
They saved him,
they saved all his sons and his wives.
And then, my father the Khan, you said to me,
"My people and possessions have been saved for me,
saved by my son, Temujin, and his four heroes."
Now my father the Khan,
what reason do you have to complain against me?
Send me a messenger stating what offense I've committed against you.' "
When Ong Khan heard these words he cried:
"Ah, what have I done?
Should I divide myself from my son?
If I do I divide myself from my solemn promises.
Should I ignore what he's said to me?
If I do I ignore my own obligations."
He paused and they could see he was deeply troubled.
When he spoke again, he swore an oath, saying:
"When I see my son,
if I harbor any evil against him
may my blood flow like this,"
and taking a knife used to sharpen arrows,
he cut the tip of his little finger.
The blood from the cut filled a small birch-bark cup
which he gave to the messengers, saying:
"Give this to my son."

Then Chingis Khan sent another message, saying:
"Say this to Anda Jamugha.
Tell him,
'Since you couldn't stand to look me in the face

you've divided me from my father the Khan.
When we were together
the first to rise each morning
would drink from our father the Khan's blue cup.
One morning when I was first to arise
I drank from it and you were jealous of me.
Now you can empty the blue cup of our father the Khan.
But how much longer will you have to drink from it?'
And then say this to Altan and Khuchar.
Say to them,
'When you deserted me did you say to yourselves,
"We'll no longer follow Temujin"
or did you say,
"We'll keep the oath we swore by deserting our Khan"?
When we acknowledged that Khuchar was the son of Nekun Taisi
and said to you,
"Khuchar, out of all of us you should be khan,"
you were unwilling.
When we said to you,
"Altan, you are the son of Khutula Khan who governed us all.
Altan, out of all of us you should be khan,"
you also refused.
When we said,
"Let's ask the sons of the sons of Okin Barkhagh,
Khabul's eldest son.
Both Sacha Beki and Taichu should be our rulers,"
I couldn't convince them to accept.
So when I said to you,
"You be our khan,"
You refused.
When you said to me,
"You be our khan,"
I agreed to govern our people.
If you had become my ruler
and I, protected by Heaven,
been ordered to ride against your enemy,
I'd have searched through the spoils for the beautiful women and virgins,

94

for the great palace tents,
for the young virgins and loveliest women,
for the finest geldings and mares.
I'd have gathered all these and brought them to you.
If I'd been told to surround the wild game of the mountains
and drive them together so that they stood leg to leg,
I'd have rounded them up for you.
If I'd been told to gather the wild game of the cliffs
and force them together so that they stood side by side,
if I'd been ordered to herd the wild game of the steppe
and bring them together so that they stood belly to belly,
I'd have done that for you.
Now you should be great supporters of my father the Khan,
but I've heard some say that your loyalty leaves much to be desired.
We don't want people to say,
"It was Temujin's leadership that made them seem like great men."
Don't allow anyone else to pitch their tents
at the head of the Three Rivers,
in our homeland where the Keluren, the Onan, and the Tula begin.'
Then take this message to Anda Senggum.
Tell him,
'I became our father's son when I was already fully clothed,
while you were born to him naked.
Our father the Khan has raised us both equally,
but you were afraid that I would replace you
and in your envy you drove me away.
Do what you can to heal the heartbreak
you've brought to our father the Khan.
Do your best to chase off his sorrows morning and night.
If you can't put aside your old jealousies
maybe it's because you want him to suffer.
Maybe even though he's still alive you say to yourself,
"I want to be khan." '
Now carry my message to each of these men,
and ask Senggum, Altan, Khuchar, and Jamugha
to send me two messengers with their replies."
Chingis gave all these messages to Arkhai Khasar and Sugegei Jegun to deliver.

When they recited their message to Senggum he answered:
"When did he ever speak of Ong Khan by saying 'my father the Khan'?
Wasn't he just as fast to call him 'the old murdering bastard'?
And when did he ever call me his 'anda'?
Wouldn't he just as soon call me 'witless fool'?
These are transparent lies and the just provocation for war.
Bilge Beki and Todogen, raise my standard for battle!
Send the geldings to pasture until they grow fat.
There's no reason to doubt we're going to war!"
So Arkhai Khasar and Sugegei Jegun left Ong Khan's camp,
but Sugegei's wife and children stayed with the Kereyid.
As the messengers rode back Sugegei's heart failed him.
He fell behind to return to his family.
Arkhai Khasar returned alone to deliver the answers to Chingis Khan.

Chingis Khan moved his camp to the shores of Lake Baljuna.
He encountered a band of the Dhorulas clan there,
and they surrendered themselves to him without fighting.
Then a Moslem trader named Asan came up the Ergune River,
driving a thousand male sheep and riding a white camel.
He came from the land of Ala Khush Digid Khuri, leader of the Onggud,
to trade for sable and squirrel furs.
When he drove his sheep down to water on the shores of Baljuna
he met Chingis Khan.

When Chingis Khan was camped at Baljuna
his own brother Khasar left his wife and three sons at Ong Khan's camp,
and taking only a few followers,
with nothing but the clothes on their backs,
they went off to join Chingis Khan.
They climbed up the ridges of Mount Kharagun Jidun,
but from there they still couldn't find his camp.
They wandered for days until their supplies were all gone
and they had nothing to eat but rawhide and sinew.
Finally they found Chingis Khan's camp at Baljuna,
and when Chingis learned the Khasar had come to join him
he was overjoyed.

The two brothers conferred and Chingis decided:
"I'll send messengers to Ong Khan."
He chose two messengers, Khaligudar and Chakhurkhan,
and told them:
"Go speak to my father the Khan and tell him,
'We bring a message from Khasar.'
Say to him,
'Khasar sent us to tell you,
"I went off to search for my elder brother.
Though I followed his tracks
I couldn't find where he'd gone.
Though I shouted his name
he couldn't hear my voice calling.
With the stars overhead and the earth as my pillow
I lie down to rest now.
My wife and my sons are with my father the Khan.
If you promise me safe passage
I'll return to the camp of my father the Khan." '
While you deliver this message we'll move in behind you
and meet on the banks of the Keluren at Arkhal Geugi.
Come back and meet us there."
After he sent out the messengers to Ong Khan
Chingis sent Jurchedei and Arkhai Khasar first as his spies,
and then followed them with his army,
riding from Lake Baljuna to Arkhal Geugi on the Keluren.
When Khaligudar and Chakhurkhan reached the Kereyid camp
they went to Ong Khan and said:
"We bring a message from Khasar,"
then recited the words that Chingis had told them.
Ong Khan had set up his tent made of gold
and was holding a feast.
When Ong Khan heard the message he told them:
"If that's how it is then let Khasar come back.
I'll send Iturgen back with you.
Iturgen is a man Khasar can trust."
So they rode off to find Khasar
until they approached Arkal Geugi

and there they saw the great army assembled.
When Iturgen saw the army he tried to ride back.
Khaligudar's horse was faster and overtook him
but Khaligudar didn't have the courage to capture Iturgen.
He only blocked Iturgen's way, boxing him in.
Chakhurkhan's horse was much slower,
and although he was almost out of range,
he fired an arrow that struck Iturgen's horse in the rear
and brought the animal down.
Then together the two messengers captured Iturgen
and brought him to Chingis Khan.
Chingis said to them:
"Take Iturgen to Khasar.
Let Khasar decide what to do with him."
When they brought Iturgen to Khasar,
without even speaking to him,
Khasar cut off his head and cast his body aside.

Then the two messengers reported to Chingis Khan, saying:
"Ong Khan doesn't suspect we're here.
He's set up his golden tent and he's holding a feast.
If we assemble our army and ride through the night
we can surround his camp and attack by surprise."
Chingis Khan agreed with this plan,
and sending Jurchedei and Arkhai Khasar in the lead,
he ordered his army to ride through the night.
They surrounded Ong Khan's camp at the mouth of the Jer Khabchighai Pass.
For three nights and three days they fought,
completely surrounding them,
until on the third day Ong Khan's army surrendered.
Somehow Ong Khan and Senggum had escaped in the night
and the warrior who had held them off was the Jirgin chief,
Khadagh the Brave.
When Khadagh surrendered he came to Chingis Khan, saying:
"I fought you three nights and three days
because I said to myself,

'How can I allow them to capture my khan
and kill him before my own eyes?'
I couldn't desert my khan
so I fought day after day, saying,
'Let him escape from here and save his own life.'
Now if you wish you can kill me.
But if Chingis Khan will let me live
I'll give him my strength."
Chingis approved of what Khadagh had done, saying:
"It's a great warrior who fights on, saying,
'I can't desert my khan until he's escaped and saved his own life.'
This is the kind of man I would have in my army."
So rather than execute Khadagh, Chingis said:
"In exchange for the life of Khuyildar
who died of the wounds he received fighting for me,
let Khadagh the Brave and the hundred best Jirgin
serve Khuyildar's wife and sons.
If the Jirgin have sons
let them serve the sons of Khuyildar.
If the Jirgin have daughters
they're not to be married.
They're to be servants for Khuyildar's wife and sons."
In memory of the service of Khuyildar,
because he offered to fight for Chingis Khan even before Jurchedei,
Chingis said:
"Because of the services Khuyildar did for me
I will provide for his orphans down to the seed of his seed."

Then they took all the Kereyid people
and dispersed them among us,
taking all their possessions as spoils.
Among them was Ong Khan's younger brother, Jakha Gambu,
and his two daughters.
Chingis took the eldest daughter, Ibakha Beki, for himself,
and gave the younger, Sorkhaghtani Beki,
to his youngest son, Tolui.

And Chingis favored Jakha Gambu,
allowing him to keep his own people,
and wouldn't allow anyone to take his possessions away.

Then Chingis Khan spoke to the two men who had saved him, saying:
"Because of what Badai and Kishiligh have done for me
I give them Ong Khan's golden tent just as it sits here,
together with the golden pitchers
and the servants to carry all the basins and bowls.
Let the Ongkhojid clan of the Kereyid become their personal guard.
Let these two men be allowed to wear quivers and drink holy wine
and let them always be free men from now on
down to the seed of their seed.
When we defeat our enemies and take our spoils
let them take whatever they want.
When we hunt for wild game
let them take as much as they want.
It was the actions of Badai and Kishiligh that saved my life.
They brought me the protection of Heaven,
allowed me to defeat the Kereyid people and sit on my throne.
Long after we're gone
let whoever sits on my throne
remember the great service these men have done
and honor them down to the seed of their seed."

So they took away the possessions of all the Kereyid people
and divided them among us so that everyone had what they wanted.
Then they divided and dispersed all the Kereyid clans,
all the ten thousand Tubegen,
the numerous Dongkhayid,
the brave Jirgin warriors.
The Kereyid people were disbanded.

Chingis Khan made his camp for the winter at Abjiga Kodeger.
Ong Khan and Senggum had not wanted to surrender themselves
and had escaped from the fighting
with nothing but the clothes on their backs.

They rode off toward the east
and when Ong Khan reached the Nekun River
he stopped there to drink.
When he came down to the river
he was captured by a Naiman soldier called Khori Subechi.
When the man seized him, he said:
"I am Ong Khan,"
but the soldier didn't believe him.
He didn't recognize that this was Ong Khan
and he killed him.

Senggum did not go down to the Nekun River
and instead rode off into the desert.
His only companions were his servants,
Kokochu, and Kokochu's wife,
and together they searched for water and food.
Finally they spotted a group of wild horses being attacked by a fly-swarm.
Senggum dismounted,
hoping to sneak up and capture a horse,
and gave his own horse to Kokochu to hold.
At that Kokochu took the bridle in his hand and rode off,
abandoning Senggum in the desert.
His wife protested, saying:
"When you were dressed in fine clothing and pieces of gold
and you ate only the finest of meats,
your lord, Senggum, called you 'my faithful Kokochu.'
How can you abandon Senggum and leave him to die like this?"
She drew up her horse and refused to ride any farther.
And Kokochu shot back at her:
"You're just thinking to yourself,
'I'll make Senggum my husband now,'
that's the only reason you want to go back to him."
"There are those who believe a woman has a face like a dog.
They say a woman is always unfaithful to her husband," she answered.
"I can't answer that,
but I ask that you at least leave him his golden cup.
At least leave him a cup to drink water from."

So Kokochu went back to where he'd left Senggum.
He threw the gold cup to the ground, crying:
"Take it!"
and rode off.
When Kokochu and his wife arrived at the camp of Chingis Khan
they told Chingis all about what they'd done.
Kokochu said:
"I've come to you after abandoning Senggum in the desert,"
and he repeated all the words that were said between himself and his wife.
Chingis Khan answered him, saying:
"This servant, Kokochu, has come to us after deserting his lord.
How could such a man ever be trusted?"
He favored Kokochu's wife because of what she'd said,
but he killed Kokochu and abandoned his body.

Gurbesu, mother of Tayang Khan of the Naiman,
sent a message to the soldier Khori Subechi, saying:
"Ong Khan was an old man and a great khan.
Bring me the head of this man that you've killed.
If it's really Ong Khan's head then we'll sacrifice to it."
Her messenger had Khori Subechi cut off the head of the corpse
and he brought it back to Gurbesu as she'd commanded.
Seeing that it was really Ong Khan's head
she placed it on a white felt carpet
and had her children's wives perform rites for it.
One girl offered it holy wine,
another played the lute for it,
and another placed before it a sacrificial bowl.
As the head was being honored this way, it laughed.
"It laughed," cried Tayang Khan,
and he smashed the skull with his feet.
The great warrior, Kogsegu Sabragh, spoke out at this, saying:
"First you order the head of a dead khan cut off and brought to you,
then you smash it.
These actions are wrong, all wrong.
Hear how the dogs bark now.
Do you hear them?

There are bad things to come.
Long ago your father, Inancha Bilge Khan, said,
'My wife is young and I have grown old.
Our son Tayang has been born only thanks to our prayers.
Can this late-born son of mine rule over my burden,
all these quarrelsome, difficult people of mine?'
Now the dogs are all barking.
This means bad things are near.
These orders our Khatun, Gurbesu, has given are sacrilege.
Your judgement is weak, late-born Tayang, my Khan.
Your wisdom and skills are good only for hunting and falconing."
But Tayang Khan ignored what he said, and instead answered:
"We hear there are very few Mongol to the east.
By shaking their quivers at the old Ong Khan they frightened him.
They made him run and now they've caused his death.
These same Mongol are saying to themselves,
'We shall be khan.'
They're saying,
'In the Heavens there are many great lights.
In the Heavens there are the sun and the moon.'
That's true.
In Heaven there are both the sun and the moon.
But on earth there can be only one khan.
We'll go to war with them and bring back the Mongol."
At this his mother, Gurbesu, said:
"But what will you do with them?
These Mongol people stink and their clothing is filthy.
They can keep their distance from us, if you please.
But perhaps if you brought their most beautiful girls,
if we could get them to wash off their hands,
we could use them to milk our cows and our sheep."
Encouraged by this Tayang Khan added:
"So you see,
why should it be difficult to conquer them?
Let's go to war with the Mongol and bring back their quivers!"
After hearing this speech, Kogsegu Sabragh said to him:
"You know how to talk big words, my Tayang Khan,

but what you say is unwise.
You'd better not say such things if you know what's good for you."
Tayang Khan ignored that warning too,
and he sent Torbi Tashi as a messenger
to find Ala Khush Digid Khuri of the Onggud, saying:
"We hear there are very few Mongol to the east.
You be my right hand and soon I will join you with an army.
We'll bring back the quivers of this small band of Mongol."
When he heard this message Ala Khush Digid Khuri replied:
"I can't be your right hand."
Then Ala Khush Digid Khuri sent his own messenger, Yokhunan,
to Chingis Khan, saying:
"Tayang Khan of the Naiman is coming to take away your quiver.
He asked me to be his right hand in this.
I won't send him my troops
and I decided to send you this message to warn you.
I'm afraid if he took you by surprise
his army would defeat you."

At this time Chingis Khan was leading a hunting party on the Steppe of the Camel.
As his party came around Tulkin Chegud,
the messenger Yokhunan met him and delivered the warning.
The Mongol called off the hunt and assembled a council.
"What can we do?" someone asked,
while others spoke up, saying:
"Our geldings are too lean from the hunting to fight.
What should we do?"
At this Prince Odchigin replied to them:
"What good is it to say 'the geldings are lean'?
After what the Naiman have said about us
how can we even sit here and talk?"
Then Prince Belgutei stood up and added:
"If a man with breath still in him
lets an enemy take his quiver
what's the point of having lived at all?
When a man dies his quiver and bow should be buried next to his bones.
That's the right way to die.

The Naiman boast how they, the most numerous people,
are also the most powerful.
If we use this boast as a just provocation to attack them by surprise,
to find them still in their camp and take the quivers off their backs,
won't that give the advantage to us?
When we attack their camp by surprise
they'll leave their huge herds behind.
When they run from their camp
they'll abandon their fine palace tents.
Their plentiful people will run from us into the mountains to escape.
Having heard these insults and threats from the Naiman
how can we continue to sit here and talk?
Let's attack them at once!"

When he returned from his hunting
Chingis Khan approved of what Prince Belgutei had said,
and moved away from Abjigha Koteger
to the Keltegi Cliffs on the Khalkha River.
Here he pitched his camp and set his army in order.
He divided the men into thousands to form troops of a thousand,
and appointed for each troop a captain of thousands,
captains of hundreds, and captains of tens.
He appointed six men to be stewards of the army,
giving them the title of Cherbi,
including Dodai and Ogele Cherbi among them.
Then having divided the army to form troops of a thousand,
having divided it further to form troops of a hundred,
having divided these further to form troops of ten,
he chose from among them his personal guard,
the eighty nightguards and seventy dayguards.
For this he inspected the sons and relations of all his captains,
and the sons and relations of all common soldiers,
and he selected those with the greatest ability,
those most fit and pleasant to look at.
He had Arkhai Khasar help him, saying:
"Let's pick the bravest men and form a troop of a thousand.
On the days of battle these will fight in front of me.

On the other days they will be my dayguard.
Ogele Cherbi will be their commander
and Khudus Khalkhan will advise him."
Then Chingis Khan established these regulations:
"Let the archers,
the soldiers of the dayguard,
the cooks,
the door keepers,
and the keepers of the geldings
each take his turn at their post during daylight.
Before sunset let the nightguards relieve them.
The men who've served me in daylight
will go spend the night with their horses.
Let the nightguard assign men to lie in the grass around my tent in the darkness,
and assign others to be the door sentries.
Then at daylight when I arise for my morning drink
let the archers and dayguards tell the nightguards they're here
and let the archers,
the soldiers who are dayguards,
the cooks, and the door keepers
each go to their job.
Let them each be seated in his proper place.
They'll each finish their assigned tasks,
which will last three days and nights,
spending each of the nights the same way with their horses,
then they'll trade places with the men who've relieved them,
becoming the nightguards on the following night,
beginning as the men who lie in the grass around my tent."

So having divided his army to form troops of a thousand,
having appointed his stewards,
having chosen his eighty nightguards,
and seventy soldiers as dayguards,
having selected the bravest among them for Arkhai Khasar to lead,
having made his camp near Keltegi Cliffs on the Khalkha,
it being the sixteenth day of the summer's first moon,
the Red Circle day in the Year of the Rat,

having sprinkled libations of mare's milk on his standard of nine tails
as a signal to Heaven that he was going to war,
Chingis Khan set out with his army against the Naiman.
Moving down the Keluren Valley
he sent Jebe and Khubilai out in the lead.
When they reached the Donkey-back Steppe near Mount Khangkharkhan
they met with the Naiman soldiers who were sentries there.
The Naiman rode after our men
and one of our soldiers,
the man had a white horse with a poor saddle on it,
was captured when his saddle broke loose.
Taking his horse, the Naiman examined it and said to themselves:
"Look at the ribs poking through.
The Mongol geldings are lean."
When our army reached the Donkey-back Steppe
they halted and a council was called.
The people asked:
"What should we do?"
Dodai Cherbi offered this plan:
"It's true they outnumber us,
but we knew that before we came to attack them.
We've exhausted ourselves from the march
so let's stop here for now.
This steppe is rich and our horses can graze awhile.
Let's pitch our tents and spread out across the whole steppe.
Let every man among us light five fires each,
and the sight of these fires will terrify them.
It's said that the Naiman are strong in numbers
but their khan is a weak man who's never been out of his tent.
While our fires confuse them our horses will fatten.
When our horses are strong we will charge at their sentries,
driving them back,
forcing their army to unite in one mass.
If we attack that way we'll have a good chance of beating them."
Chingis Khan approved this plan
and he ordered his soldiers, saying:
"Let each of you light five fires."

They spread themselves across the Donkey-back Steppe
pitching their tents far apart
and each man lit fires in five different places.
That night the sentries on Mount Khangkharkhan looked down on all of the fires
and sent word to Tayang Khan, saying:
"It's said there are very few Mongol
but they have more fires than the stars in the sky."
They sent him the little white horse with the poor saddle they'd captured, saying:
"The Mongol soldiers have pitched their tents
and cover the Donkey-back Steppe.
Each day their number seems to increase.
They have more fires now than the stars in the sky."
This message reached Tayang Khan
while he was camped on the Khachir River in the mountains of Khanghai.
Thinking it over,
he sent a message to his son, Gughlug Khan, saying:
"The Mongol horses are lean.
Our sentries say,
'They have more fires than stars in the sky.'
This means the Mongol are numerous.
If we attack them now it will be hard to beat them.
If we attack them now they won't even flinch.
These Mongol are the kind of warriors who won't retreat
even though an arrow has pierced through their cheek,
even when black blood flows from their wounds.
Would attacking them now be a wise thing to do?
Now it's said that the Mongol horses are lean.
If we were to take our people back over the Altai,
retreating in order this way,
reforming our army on the other side of the passes,
marching back and enticing them to follow us,
appearing to retreat from them
but still fighting small skirmishes along the way
until we reach the foot of the Altai. . . .
Right now our geldings are too fat for battle.
Such a march would pull up their bellies
and make them ready for war.

The Mongol horses will be exhausted by then
and we'll throw our army back in their faces."
Hearing these words, Gughlug Khan answered him:
"Ah, Tayang, he talks like a woman!
His heart is so weak.
Where would these numerous Mongol have come from?
Most of the Mongol are with Jamugha
and he's here with us.
Tayang's timid little heart
which has gone no farther from his tent
than where a pregnant woman pisses,
which has gone no farther toward the pasture
than a calf tied to the wheel of a cart,
this woman's heart has already failed him.
That's why he sent me this cowardly plan."
And Gughlug Khan sent this speech by messenger to his father,
knowing full well what he said would injure his father's pride.
Hearing his own son compare him to a woman, Tayang Khan replied:
"Well, let the mighty Gughlug,
the courageous Gughlug,
on the day when the Mongol and Naiman meet to kill one another
not lose this courage he feels so strongly today.
When the Mongol and the Naiman meet head-on in battle
it won't be easy to beat them."
And when Khori Subechi,
the great captain who governed under Tayang Khan,
heard what Tayang had said to his son,
he spoke out, saying:
"Your father, Inancha Bilge Khan,
never turned his back or showed the rear of his horse
to a man he knew to be his equal in war.
Yet now, before we even get started, your heart gives out.
If we'd known that your heart was so weak
we'd have brought out your mother, Gurbesu,
even though she's a woman,
and had her command the army.
Why must our people suffer for the fact that your father grew old?

The discipline in our army is lax.
It's the time of the Mongol.
I can see it.
Destiny's with them now, not us.
Late-born Tayang, as a leader you're useless,"
and striking his quiver in disgust Khori Subechi rode off.
When Tayang Khan heard this he grew angry and said:
"Every life ends in death,
every body feels pain.
We all share this fate.
If now is the time to attack the Mongol
then we'll fight them."
He gathered his people from the banks of the Khachir
and the Naiman swept down the Tamir River Valley,
crossing the Orkhon,
passing the eastern edge of Mount Nakhu.
As they came to the Chakirmagud they were seen by Chingis Khan's sentries.
Our sentries rode off, crying:
"The Naiman army's reached Chakirmagud!"
When this news reached him
Chingis Khan assembled his army and spoke to them, saying:
"This will be a great battle.
This will be a decisive one.
We may lose everything or we may lose only a few.
We must set out against the Naiman in strictest order.
Taking kharaghana formation
we'll march in close rank like a thorny shrub.
Then advancing in lake array
we'll spread out like the waters filling the steppe.
Finally charging together at the center of their army
we'll drive through their lines like a chisel through wood."
Chingis himself took command of the foward troops
then he made Khasar commander of the army of the center,
and Prince Odchigin commander of the horses in reserve.

Our forward troops drove the Naiman sentries back from Chakirmagud
Their forces retreated from us,

reforming before Mount Nakhu
on the skirts of the mountains there.
Our forward troops drove them back,
herding them together into a great mass before Mount Nakhu.
Tayang Khan saw the Mongol driving his soldiers before them,
and he turned to Jamugha,
who had gathered his army and joined with the Naiman,
and Tayang Khan asked Jamugha:
"What are these people who charge at us
like wolves pursuing so many sheep,
chasing the sheep right into the flock?"
And Jamugha replied:
"My friend, Anda Temujin, has fed four dogs with human flesh,
then held them back with iron chains.
These are the people who charge at us,
pursuing our soldiers.
These four dogs have helmets of copper,
snouts like chisels,
tongues like awls,
hearts of iron,
whips sharp as swords.
These four dogs feed on the dew and ride on the winds.
These four, when they fight an enemy, feed on his flesh.
These four take human flesh as their share of the spoils.
Now he's cast off their chains and set them on us.
He's let them loose and they charge at us,
mad with joy,
their hungry mouths foaming."
And when he asked:
"These four dogs, who are they?"
Jamugha replied:
"These four are Jebe and Khubilai,
Jelme and Subetei."
"Let's move away from these creatures," Tayang Khan said,
and riding back, he halted where the steppe meets the mountains.
From here he looked back and saw new soldiers close behind the first ones,
riders making their horses leap and gallop in circles,

closing in behind them,
and Tayang Khan asked Jamugha:
"Who are these people?
How can they ride in circles around our soldiers,
leaping like foals let loose at morning play,
like foals full of milk from their mother's teats,
playing merrily in the pasture?"
And Jamugha replied:
"These are the Urugud and Manghud clans,
who charge into the lancebearers,
then strip the clothes from their corpses.
They drive the swordsmen before them
and cut them down from their horses,
stripping off their clothes and possessions as part of the spoils.
That must be who you see
leaping and galloping into battle now."
And Tayang Khan spoke again, saying:
"Let's move back away from these creatures,"
and he rode further back, now ascending the mountainside.
Looking down, he turned to Jamugha and asked:
"Who are these troops
cutting like a sword through the ranks,
crying like falcons who must have their food,
swooping towards us?"
Jamugha replied:
"These are Temujin's troops.
Anda Temujin is coming.
He's so covered with armor
an awl beaten from copper couldn't find a space to pierce it,
a needle hammered from iron couldn't slip between its plates.
Temujin swoops down on us like a falcon hungry for food.
The Naiman were saying that when they saw the Mongol they'd devour them,
there wouldn't even be a scrap of goat hair left behind.
Now look at them."
Hearing these words, Tayang Khan spoke, saying:
"These are terrible men,
frightening men.

Let's ride further up the mountain and stand there,"
and he rode further up Mount Nakhu.
Again Tayang Khan turned to Jamugha and asked:
"And who's this?
Who charges behind Temujin?"
And Jamugha replied:
"Mother Hogelun weaned one of her sons with human flesh.
He's as tall as three men,
can make a meal of a three-year-old cow,
and wears a breast plate that's three layers thick.
He rides out on a cart drawn by three bulls.
If he were to swallow a soldier and all his weapons
it wouldn't even fill up his mouth.
Swallowing whole men doesn't satisfy his hunger.
If he's angry
and draws back his bow to shoot a fork-tipped arrow,
it will pierce right through ten or twenty men,
even though they're on the far side of a mountain.
If he draws on his bow and shoots a single-tipped arrow,
it skewers all the soldiers who come out to fight him,
even though they're at the far side of the steppe.
If he draws on his bow and shoots with all of his strength
he'll hit a man nine hundred yards away.
If he draws on his bow no stronger than other men do
he'll hit a man at five hundred yards.
There's no one who can match him in battle.
He's called Khasar and he's fierce as a python.
That's who's charging at us now."
Then Tayang Khan spoke out, saying:
"If that's so,
then let's head for the heights of the mountain,"
and ascending the mountain further,
he looked back at the battle.
Then turning to Jamugha he asked:
"Who's this now behind Khasar?"
Jamugha replied:
"This is Odchigin,

Mother Hogelun's youngest son.
He's said to be the lazy one,
the first one to sleep and the last one to rise.
But even he doesn't stay behind.
Even he comes charging at us in the battle."
Tayang Khan spoke, saying:
"If that's so then let's ride for the top of the mountain."
After he'd said all this to Tayang Khan
Jamugha deserted the Naiman and escaped from the battle alone.
Before he made his escape
he sent a messenger to Chingis Khan.
"Speak to Anda Temujin," he told the messenger,
and he sent these words:
"After hearing how I spoke about you
Tayang Khan was terrified.
He's retreated from you up the mountainside.
He's been killed by the words from my mouth.
He's lost what judgment he had and has ridden up the mountain.
Be careful, my friend.
The Naiman have fled from you up into the highlands.
They don't have the nerve to show their faces before you.
As for me,
I've separated myself from the Naiman."

As twilight fell Chingis Khan ordered his army to halt,
and they passed that night surrounding Mount Nakhu.
In the darkness
the Naiman tried to drive their carts and horses back down
and fell from the cliffs and narrow trails of Nakhu,
their bodies falling atop one another,
their bones shattering from the fall,
their bodies crushing each other like piles of dead trees,
and that's how most of them died.
At daybreak they put an end to Tayang Khan.
Tayang's son, Gughlug, ran away
and was overtaken near the Tamir River.
He threw up a fort there with a few of his followers,

but unable to hold out against us
they fled out into the desert.
The Naiman people were assembled at the foot of the Altai
and were disposed of.
The Mongol clans who were with Jamugha:
the Dorben, the Tayichigud, the Ungirad,
the Jadaran, the Khatagin, and the Saljigud,
all these people surrendered to us there.
Lastly Chingis Khan commanded that Gurbesu, Tayang's mother,
be brought before him.
He spoke to her, saying:
"It was you who said,
'The Mongol stink and their clothing is filthy.
If we could make their most beautiful girls wash their hands
they'd only be fit to milk our cows and our sheep.'
Then why are you here?'"
And Chingis Khan took her as one of his wives.

In the fall of that same Year of the Rat
Chingis Khan led his armies against the remaining followers of Toghtoga Beki,
who had fled to the Kharadal Forest.
He forced Toghtoga to retreat,
driving his people out onto the Donkey-back Steppe,
capturing all his herds and possessions.
Toghtoga, along with his sons Khudu and Chilagun,
with a few followers and nothing but the clothes on their backs,
escaped from the battle and got away.

After the main body of the Merkid were defeated
the Merkid clan chief, Dayir Usun,
decided to come out from the forest to surrender.
He rode out with his daughter, Khulan Khatun, saying:
"I'll offer her as a present to Chingis Khan."
But the steppe was still full of soldiers
roaming about and blocking their way.
They met the Mongol commander, Nayaga,
and Dayir Usun told him:

"I've come out to surrender to Chingis Khan and tell him,
'I offer you my daughter as a present.' "
   Nayaga took him back to his own tent, saying:
"We'll present her to Chingis Khan together.
   Our men are still at war with the Merkid.
   If you go off alone
   they'll kill you and take your daughter."
   He kept Dayir Usun in his tent for three days and nights,
   then he brought the Merkid chief and Khulan Khatun to Chingis Khan.
   Chingis heard Nayaga's words and grew furious:
"Why did you keep her in your tent for three nights?
   Your punishment will be an example to everyone.
   I will not tolerate such behavior from any man."
   Then Khulan Khatun spoke up to defend him, saying:
"Nayaga spoke to us and warned us.
'I'm one of Chingis Khan's commanders,' he said.
'If you travel alone the soldiers will give you trouble.'
   If we'd met up with any soldiers but those commanded by Nayaga
   would we ever have reached you unharmed?
   So the fact that we met up with Nayaga is very fortunate.
   Now, if instead of asking Nayaga why he kept me for three nights,
   if the Khan will ask me,
   if he'll examine my maidenhead,
   which by the grace of Heaven is no different now
   than the day I was born to my parents,
   he'll see that I am untouched by any man."
   And Nayaga answered for himself, saying:
"I have no face other than the one devoted to my Khan.
   When I find beautiful women and virgins,
   when I find powerful geldings and mares among foreign people,
   I say to myself,
'These are the possessions of my Khan.'
   If I've ever thought anything else then put me to death."
   Chingis Khan accepted what Khulan Khatun had said.
   That very day he examined her and slept with her,
   and after finding that everything she'd said was true
   he was happy to take her as one of his wives.

116

He said of Nayaga:
"Here is an honest man.
I'll give great responsibilities to a man like this."

The Merkid people's possessions were taken away
and Chingis Khan captured the wives of Khudu, Toghtoga's son.
One of these noblewomen, named Doregene,
he gave to his son Ogodei as a wife.
Half the remaining Merkid continued to fight us,
and fell back to a fort they'd built in the high mountain woods.
Chingis Khan sent the troops of the Left Hand
under the command of Chimbai, Sorkhan Shira's son,
to attack the Merkid who resisted,
and he led another army himself in pursuit of Toghtoga
and his sons Khudu and Chilagun,
who had escaped with a few followers
and nothing but the clothes on their backs.
These forces spent the winter at the base of the Altai,
then in the spring of the Year of the Ox,
Chingis Khan rode off past the settlement at Alai,
capturing the people of Guchlug Khan, the Naiman prince,
and Guchlug, escaping with a few followers,
joined forces with Toghtoga the Merkid on the banks of the Irtysh.
When the two forces met in battle
Toghtoga was knocked from his horse by an arrow.
His sons were unable to bury him there
and they had no time to carry his body away.
So they cut off his head to honor it later and fled.
The Naiman and Merkid forces weren't able to withstand the attack
and they tried to retreat across the Irtysh River,
swollen by spring floods.
Many men sank into the waters and drowned there.
The few that survived crossing the river dispersed.
Guchlug Khan escaped from the battle,
passing by the land of the Uighur and Kharlukhs,
and finally joined forces with the Gur Khan of Black Cathay
on the Chui River in the land of the Moslems.

The Merkid led by Toghtoga's sons Khudu, Khal, and Chilagun
fled past the land of the Khanghli and the Kipchakh peoples.
By the time Chingis Khan returned with his forces
Chimbai had defeated the Merkid in the high mountain woods.
Chingis ordered that some of the Merkid be killed
and the rest were stripped of their possessions.
But even these survivors rose up against us in the Great Camp
so that our servants had to subdue them again.
This time Chingis Khan made a decree, saying:
"In the past we've said,
'Let them live as a tribe.'
But these people continue to resist us."
He ordered that the Merkid be disbanded,
distributing their people among all the other divisions,
so that they ceased to exist as a people.

During the same Year of the Ox
Chingis Khan sent out Subetei,
equipping his army with iron carts,
to pursue the sons of Toghtoga Beki and their followers.
He sent Subetei off with this message:
"Toghtoga's sons Khudu, Khal, and Chilagun have run from us,
mad with fear,
turning to shoot at us and running again,
hysterical like wild horses who feel the noose on their necks,
like deer already wounded by arrows.
If they sprout wings and fly up toward Heaven,
you, Subetei, become a falcon and seize them in mid-air.
If they become marmots and claw into the Earth with their nails,
you become an iron rod and bore through the Earth to catch them.
If they become fish and dive into the depths of the Sea,
you, Subetei, become a net,
casting yourself over them and dragging them back.
I'm sending you off to cross high passes and ford great rivers.
Keep in mind the distance you'll have to travel
and spare your horses so they don't get exhausted.
Conserve their strength before it's used up.

When a gelding is already worn out, it's useless to spare him.
Once you've used up all your provisions there's nothing to save.
There'll be a great deal of game to hunt on the way.
Keep in mind how far you have to go
and don't let your men ride off to hunt at their whim.
Only hunt within limits.
When you decide to hunt tell your men,
'We will hunt now to provide food for the army,'
then set a limit on how much will be killed.
See to it that your men keep their crupper hanging loose on their mounts
and the bit of their bridle out of the mouth,
except when you allow them to hunt.
That way they won't be able to simply gallop off at their whim.
Having established these rules
see to it you seize and beat any man who breaks them.
Any man that I know who ignores my decree,
have him brought back to stand before me.
Any man I don't know who ignores this decree,
cut off his head where he stands.
Though your army will divide beyond the great rivers
all must continue in pursuit of one goal.
Though mountain ranges separate your men from each other
think of nothing else but this task.
If your ability and powers are strengthened by Eternal Heaven,
if your power is great enough to lay hands on the sons of Toghtoga Beki,
it would serve no purpose to bring them back to me.
Just kill them."
And Chingis Khan said to Subetei:
"I am sending you off to war now
because in my youth the three Merkid chiefs frightened me.
They chased me three times around Burkhan Khaldun.
Now these hateful people,
hurling insults at me and swearing never to surrender,
these people have tried to run away from me.
Follow them to the ends of the earth,
find them at the bottom of the sea."
So in the Year of the Ox

he sent Subetei off in pursuit of the Merkid rebels,
having the blacksmiths beat out iron carts for the army,
ordering Subetei to follow them to the ends of the Earth.
And Chingis Khan made this decree:
"If you go to war with this in mind,
that though I'm out of your sight
it's as if you can still see me,
that though I'm far away
it's as if I'm near at hand,
then the Eternal Blue Heaven will protect you as well."

When Chingis Khan defeated the Naiman army
Jamugha had been with the Naiman
and in the battle all of his people were taken away.
He had escaped with only five followers
and become a bandit in the Tangnu Mountains.
One day he and his companions were lucky enough to kill a great mountain sheep,
and as they sat around the fire roasting the mutton
Jamugha said to his companions:
"What nobleman's sons are so lucky today
to have such a feast of roast mutton to eat?"
But even as he said this
his five followers seized him,
and binding Jamugha they brought him to Chingis Khan.
Because he'd been captured this way, Jamugha said:
"Tell my anda, the Khan,
'Black crows have captured a beautiful duck.
Peasants and slaves have laid hands on their lord.
My anda the Khan will see this and know what to do.
Brown vultures have captured a mandarin duck.
Slaves and servants have conspired against their lord.
Surely my holy anda will know how to respond to this.' "
When he heard Jamugha's words Chingis Khan made a decree:
"How can we allow men who lay hands on their own lord to live?
Who could trust people like this?
Such people should be killed
along with all their descendants!"

He brought before Jamugha the men who had seized him,
these men who had betrayed their own lord,
and in their lord's presence their heads were cut off.
  Then Chingis Khan said:
"Tell Jamugha this.
 'Now we two are together.
Let's be allies.
Once we moved together like the two shafts of a cart,
but you thought about separating from me and you left.
Now that we're together again in one place
let's each be the one to remind the other of what he forgot;
let's each be the one to awaken the other's judgment whenever it sleeps.
Though you left me you were always my anda.
On the day when we met on the battlefield
the thought of trying to kill me brought pain to your heart.
Even though you went your own way
the day when we met as enemies in war
the thought that I would die brought you pain.
If you ask me, "When did this happen?"
I'll tell you it was when I met the Kereyid at the sands of Khalakhaljid.
You sent me a messenger
to inform me about what you'd said to our father, Ong Khan.
That was the service you did for me there.
Then again when we fought with the Naiman
you sent me a messenger telling me how you'd terrified the Naiman.
They were killed by your mouth;
your words made them die.
You told me their own fear would kill them.
That was the service you did for me there.' "
  Jamugha answered him:
"Long ago when we were children in the Khorkhonagh Valley
I declared myself to be your anda.
Together we ate the food which is never digested
and spoke words to each other which are never forgotten,
and at night we shared one blanket to cover us both.
Then it was as if people came between us with knives,
slashing our legs and stabbing our sides,

and we were separated from each other.
I thought to myself,
'We've made solemn promises to each other'
and my face was so blackened by the winds of shame
that I couldn't bring myself to show my face,
this shameful windburned face,
before the warm face of my anda, the Khan.
I thought to myself,
'We've spoken words to each other that are never forgotten'
and my face was so red from the heat of my shame
that I went far away from you,
unable to show this burned, peeling face
before the clear face of my anda, whose memory is long.
And now my anda, the Khan wants to favor me,
and says to me, 'Let's be allies.'
When I should have been his ally I deserted him.
Now, my anda, you've pacified every nation;
you've united every tribe in the world.
The Great Khan's throne has given itself to you.
Now that the world is ready for you
what good would I be as your ally?
I'd only invade your dreams in the dark night
and trouble your thoughts in the day.
I'd be like a louse on your collar,
like a thorn under your shirt.
I was brought up by my father's grandmothers.
I went wrong when I strove to be a better man than my anda.
In this life, of the two of us,
it's my name that's reached from sunrise to sunset;
it's Jamugha who's reached the end of his days.
My anda has a wise mother.
Having been born a great hero,
he has skillful young brothers.
Having many fine men by his side,
he's always been greater than I am.
As for me,
since I lost both my parents when I was young,

I have no younger brothers.
My wife is a babbling fool.
I can't trust the men at my side.
Because of all this
my anda, whose destiny is Heaven's will,
has surpassed me in everything.
My anda, if you want to favor me,
then let me die quickly and you'll be at peace with your heart.
When you have me killed, my anda,
see that it's done without shedding my blood.
Once I am dead and my bones have been buried high on a cliff
I will protect your seed and the seed of your seed.
I will become a prayer to protect you.
My very nature is different than yours.
I've been crushed by my anda's generosity and greatness.
Remember these words that I've spoken
and repeat them to each other morning and night.
Now let me die quickly."
Hearing this Chingis Khan spoke:
"Though my anda deserted me
and said many things against me,
I've never heard that he ever wanted me dead.
He's a man we all might learn from
but he's not willing to stay with us.
If I simply ordered him to be killed
there isn't a diviner in the world who could justify it.
If I harmed this man's life without good reason
it would bring a curse on us.
Jamugha is a noble and important man.
You can speak to him and give him this reason.
Tell him,
'One time in the past
because Jochi Darmala and Taichar stole a herd of horses from one another,
Anda Jamugha, you broke your oath
and attacked me at Seventy Marshes.
I was forced to run from you there,
retreating to the refuge of Jerene Narrows.

That time you put fear in my heart.
Now I say "Let's be allies" but you refuse me.
When I try to spare your life you won't allow it.'
So speak to Jamugha and tell him,
'Allow this man to kill you
according to your own wishes,
without shedding your blood.' "
And Chingis Khan made a decree, saying:
"Execute Jamugha without shedding his blood
and bury his bones with all due honor."
He had Jamugha killed and his bones properly buried.

The Developing Empire

And so in the Year of the Tiger,
having set in order the lives
of all the people whose tents are protected by skirts of felt,
the Mongol clans assembled at the head of the Onan.
They raised a white standard of nine tails
and proclaimed Chingis Khan the Great Khan.
Mukhali was given the title Gui Ong, meaning Prince of the Realm
and Jebe was sent off to war against Guchulug Khan of the Naiman.
Chingis Khan set the lives of all the Mongolian peoples in order
and made this decree:
"To reward those who've fought with me to establish the Nation
I will make them Mingghan-u Noyan,
rulers of one thousand households."
He established the Mingghan-u Noyan and named them as follows:
Father Munglig, Bogorchu, Mukhali Gui Ong,
Khorchi, Ilugei, Jurchedei,
Dhunan, Khubilai, Jelme,
Tuge, Degei, Tolon,
Onggur, Chulgetei, Boroghul,
Shigi Khutukhu, Guchu, Kokochu,
Khorghosun, Husun, Khuyildar,
Shilugei, Jetei, Taghai,
Chaghagan Khoga, Alagh, Sorkhan Shira,
Bulughan, Kharachar, Koko Chos,
Suyiketu, Nayaga, Jungshoi,
Guchugur, Bala, Oronartai,
Dayir, Muge, Bujir,
Munggugur, Dologadai, Bogen,
Khudus, Maral, Jebke,

Yurukhan, Koko, Jebe,
Udutai, Bala Cherbi, Kete,
Subetei, Mungke, Khalja,
Khurchakhus, Geugi, Badai,
Kishiligh, Ketei, Chagurkhai,
Onggiran, Toghon Temur, Megetu,
Khadagan, Morokha, Dori Bukha,
Idughadai, Shiraghul, Dagun,
Tamachi, Khaguran, Alchi,
Tobsakha, Tungkhuidai, Tobukha,
Ajinai, Tuyuideger, Sechegur, Jeder,
and eight who also had the title Guregen,
meaning they had married one of Chingis Khan's daughters:
Olar Guregen, Kinggiyadai Bukha Guregen,
Khuril Ashigh Guregen, Khadai Guregen, Chigu Guregen.
Alchi Guregen was given three thousand Ongirad,
Butu Guregen two thousand Ikires,
and Ala Khush Digid Khuri five thousand of the Onggud.
All together, with the exception of the People of the Forest,
these men were named rulers of ninety-five thousand households.

As Chingis Khan was rewarding the people who had served him,
naming the captains of thousands led by Bogorchu and Mukhali,
his adopted brother, Shigi Khutukhu was in his tent.
He told Shigi Khutukhu:
"Go call for the others to come to my tent,"
and Shigi Khutukhu answered him:
"Of Bogorchu, Mukhali, and all the others
who's served you the best?
Of all of these men
who's given you more of his strength?
I haven't served less than any other man.
I haven't been less devoted.
I've grown up in your tent since I was in my cradle.
Now this much beard grows on my chin
and all that time I've thought of no one but you.
I've grown up in your golden tent since I was in diapers.

Now this much beard grows on my mouth
and all that time I've done nothing wrong.
Our mother brought me up as her son
and made me lie at her feet.
She brought me up as your younger brother
and made me lie at her side.
What rewards will you give to me?"
When Chingis Khan heard this he said:
"Are you not my sixth younger brother?
Shigi Khutukhu, my late-born brother,
you'll receive the shares due the members of my family.
And because of your services to me
you may break the law nine times
and each time you'll be pardoned."
Then Chingis Khan made this decree:
"As I stand here under the protection of Eternal Blue Heaven,
setting all of the people in order,
Shigi Khutukhu will be my eyes for seeing and my ears for hearing,
dividing the people
giving a part to our Mother,
a part to Us,
a part to our younger brothers,
and a part to our sons,
according to the names of the people,
dividing those people who live in tents protected by skirts of felt
from those living in tents whose doors are made of wood.
Let no man violate his word."
He made Shigi Khutukhu the judge of all the people,
commanding him to strike fear in the hearts of thieves,
bring remorse to the tongues of liars,
execute those whom custom has condemned to death,
and punish all those whom custom insists should be punished.
Chingis Khan made him the judge of all the people, saying:
"Let him write everything in a blue book,
recording how he's divided the people,
recording how he's judged the people,
and for all generations

let no one change anything Shigi Khutukhu,
after taking counsel with me,
has written on the white paper of his blue book.
Let no man who comes after us alter it."
After Shigi Khutukhu heard this he replied:
"How can a late-born younger brother accept
a part equal to your other brothers?
Let the Khan reward me with things he takes from earthen-walled cities."
And Chingis Khan answered him:
"Then you've named your own reward."
With that Shigi Khutukhu asked nothing more for himself
and went out to call Bogorchu, Mukali, and the others into the tent.

Then Chingis Khan spoke to Father Munglig and made this decree:
"You, my old and good friend,
you who were born at the same time I was born
and who has grown up together with me,
how many times have you served and protected me?
I remember one time when my father Ong Khan and Anda Senggum,
plotting against me,
called me to their camp,
and on the way I passed the night in the tent of Father Munglig.
If you hadn't convinced me to turn back
I would have been drowned in the whirlpool,
I would have been consumed by the fire.
With that service in mind
how could I ever forget you?
With that service in mind
I'll have you sit on a seat at the corner of my throne
and I'll ask you the meaning of the month and the year.
I'll give you favors and gifts
and I will serve you for generations to come."

Then Chingis Khan spoke to Bogorchu and made this decree:
"When I was young and thieves stole my eight horses,
I had been chasing them three days and nights when we met.
You said to me,

'I see you're in trouble and I'll help you,'
and without even telling your father,
leaving the milk bucket and milk pail in the grass,
replacing my straw-yellow horse
with a grayish-white horse with a black stripe down its back,
riding your own swift dun-colored horse
and leaving your own herd unprotected,
you set off to help me.
We rode for three days and nights across the steppe
until we came to the camp of the men who had stolen my horses,
and we drove the horses out of their camp and brought them back.
Your father is Nakhu the Rich.
You are his only son
and you became my companion for no other reason than the courage in your heart.
After that adventure I thought of you often
and finally sent Belgutei to ask you to be my companion.
You mounted your straw-yellow horse,
tied your gray felt cloak to your saddle
and rode off to join me.
When we were attacked by the three Merkid chiefs
who chased me three times around Mount Burkhan Khaldun,
you rode with me around the mountain.
Then later when we fought the Tatar at Seventy Felt Cloaks,
when we spent the night so close by the enemy
that it was as if we propped each other up,
and the rain fell on us day and night,
all through the night you covered me from the rain,
shielding me while you stood exposed
and only once shifted your feet.
That was a sign of the courage you possess.
How many more tales of your courage could I tell?
Both Bogorchu and Mukhali
by drawing out my good judgments
and blocking anything I might have done wrong,
by bringing forward the good and stopping the bad,
have brought me to sit on this throne.
Now let them both sit above all the others

and though they break the law nine times
they'll be absolved of all punishment.
Let Bogorchu rule over the ten thousand people to the south of the Altai,
all those people who sleep with the Altai mountains as their pillow."

Then Chingis Khan spoke to Mukhali and made this decree:
"When we pitched our camp in the Khorkhonagh Valley
under the Great Branching Tree where Khutula Khan danced,
you came to me with a clear message from Heaven.
Because of that message from Heaven,
thinking of your father Gugun,
I gave my word to Mukhali.
I promised him,
'You'll be placed on a high seat
and you and your descendants
will be known as Gui Ong,
Prince of the Realm by all of the people.'
So I've given the title Gui Ong to Mukhali.
Let Mukhali Gui Ong rule over the ten thousand people to the north,
all those people who sleep with the Kharagun-chidun mountains as their pillow."

Then Chingis Khan spoke to Khorchi and made this decree:
"You once came to me with a prophetic dream
and from the time I was young until now
you've suffered through the rain and the cold with me,
acting like my own guardian spirit.
When Khorchi came to tell me his dream he said,
'If my prophecy is fulfilled
and by the grace of Heaven everything happens as you want,
then favor me with thirty wives.'
Now since everything you predicted has come to pass I'll repay you.
Look for yourself among all the people who've surrendered to us
and choose the thirty best women and girls for your wives."
And to this he added the following decree:
"In addition to the Bagarin, the Chinos, and the Adarkin people,
the ten thousand people I've given him,
let Khorchi make his camp on the banks of the Irtysh River

and let all the People of the Forest who live by this river be his subjects.
Let no one among the People of the Forest act
without first asking Khorchi's permission.
And no man doubt that if he acts without permission
Khorchi will have such a man killed."

Then Chingis Khan spoke to Jurchedei and made this decree:
"When we were fighting the Kereyid at the Sands of Khalakhaljid
and I was unsure and anxious about the battle,
I turned to you and you swore an oath with Anda Khuyildar.
You performed great service for me, Jurchedei,
defeating the charge of the Jirgin, the Tubegen, and the Dongkhayid troops,
driving back Khuri Shilemun who led a thousand dayguards,
charging into the middle of their army.
Then by the grace of Everlasting Heaven
you fired an arrow through the cheek of Senggum,
and the doors were opened for me
and the reins were placed in my hands.
If Senggum hadn't been wounded how would that battle have ended?
Jurchedei performed a great service there.
When we divided our troops and rode along the Khalkha River,
the thought of Jurchedei by my side
was like the thought of a high mountain shelter.
When we rejoined our troops
our beasts shared the waters of Lake Baljuna.
Then when we set out from Lake Baljuna against the Kereyid
Jurchedei was sent first as a spy
and we destroyed the Kereyid people,
increasing our strength by Heaven and Earth.
Once we'd defeated all these armies
the Naiman and Merkid people didn't have the courage to face us.
We defeated and dispersed them all.
In the battles with the Naiman and Merkid,
Jakha Gambu the Kereyid surrendered to us,
offering his two daughters,
and we let him keep his own people to rule.
But he left us and became our enemy a second time.

It was Jurchedei who trapped him when he tried to escape us,
captured Jakha Gambu and executed him.
This was Jurchedei's second great service to me."
Because Jurchedei had offered his life for him on the day of battle,
because he'd been willing to fight to the death on the battlefield,
Chingis Khan gave him Ibakha Beki, Jakha Gambu's daughter.
He spoke to Ibakha, saying:
"I don't do this because you are without warmth and good sense,
nor because there is anything lacking in your beauty and charm.
I am giving you to Jurchedei,
you who have entered my heart,
who have taken your place among the line of my wives,
I am giving you to him
because of the great principle of reward for service.
On the day of the battle Jurchedei was my shield.
When I went against the enemy he was my shelter.
He united all the people who'd scattered
and gathered together all the people who'd gone separate ways.
Long after we're gone,
when my descendants sit on this throne,
let them bear in mind the principle of rewarding those who've served them
and respect my wishes to still honor the descendants of Ibakha
as though she still had her place in the line of my wives."
Then Chingis Khan spoke to Ibakha again, saying,
"Your father Jakha Gambu gave you two hundred slaves
and the cooks Ashigh Temur and Alchigh as your dowry.
Now when you leave me to go to the Urugud people
leave behind one hundred of your slaves and the cook Ashigh as a remembrance."
And Chingis Khan spoke to Jurchedei and made this decree:
"I am giving you my wife Ibakha.
May you govern wisely all the Urugud people."

Then Chingis Khan spoke to Khubilai and made this decree:
"You've pressed at the necks of mighty soldiers in my service,
you've brought down the mounts of strong men.
When I sent for my four dogs,
my Khubilai, Jelme, Jebe, and Subetei,

ordering you to go out against what I saw before me,
you were there shattering the stones when I said, 'Go there!'
You rode out smashing the cliffs the moment I said, 'Attack!'
breaking the brightest gems into pieces
and cutting the deep waters in two.
On the day of battle if I could send my four dogs,
Khubilai, Jelme, Jebe, and Subetai,
off to a place I could point to,
if I had my four heroes,
Bogorchu, Mukhali, Boroghul, and Chilagun the Brave,
there at my side,
if I had both Jurchedei and Khuyildar standing before me
leading the Urugud and the Manghud,
I had no cause for worry or fear.
Khubilai, will you take charge of the affairs of the army?
And because of his stubbornness
I haven't appointed Bedugun to be a captain of thousands.
Let him command a thousand with you, following your advice,
and we'll see how well he can do."

Then Chingis Khan spoke to Ghunan and made this decree:
"You chiefs led by Bogochu and Mukhali
and you stewards led by Dodai and Dokholhu,
listen to the wisdom of Ghunan of the Geniges.
In the night he's like a cunning wolf
and in the bright day he's like a black crow.
When we're travelling he doesn't stay camped
and when we're camped he doesn't travel.
He doesn't show one face to our friends
and a separate face to our enemies.
Don't do anything without the counsel of Ghunan and Koko Chos."
And Chingis Khan made this decree:
"Jochi is my eldest son.
Let Ghunan rule over the Geniges
and be a captain of ten thousand under Jochi."
Chingis Khan recognized that the four
who wouldn't hide from him what they'd seen,

who wouldn't conceal from him what they'd heard
were Ghunan, Koko Chos, Degei, and Old Man Usun.

Then Chingis Khan spoke to Jelme and made this decree:
"When Jelme was still in the cradle
his father, Old Man Jarchigudai came down from Mount Burkhan Khaldun.
He carried his blacksmith bellows on his back,
and gave my parents a sable blanket to wrap me in
when I was born by Deligun Hill on the Onan.
From that day Jelme has been my companion,
a servant at my threshold,
a private slave at my door.
He's performed many services for me.
This man who was born at the same time I was born,
who grew up at the same time I grew up,
has been my companion because his father wrapped me in a sable blanket.
If the fortunate Jelme were to break the law nine times
each time he'll be absolved from all punishment."

Then Chingis Khan spoke to the cook Onggur and made this decree:
"You led one of my camping circles.
You never strayed in the mists
nor left my side to follow another.
You suffered with me through the wet and the cold.
Now what rewards would you take for yourself?"
Onggur replied to him:
"My Bayagud brothers are scattered among each of the tribes.
If Chingis Khan wishes to reward me,
then allow me to collect my Bayagud brothers together."
And Chingis Khan made this decree:
"Let the cooks Onggur and Boroghul
distribute the food to the left and the right sides.
Let no one standing or seated go without food on the right;
let no one in place or out of place in the line go without food on the left.
If you two distribute the food then my mind is at rest.
So, now go and distribute the food to the people,
setting all the provisions on the great wine table.

You'll sit with the Mingghan-u Noyan
with your faces turned toward the north."
And Chingis Khan pointed out where they should sit.

Then Chingis Khan spoke to Boroghul and made this decree:
"My mother took you four,
Shigi Khutukhu, Boroghul, Guchu, and Kokochu,
from other tribe's camps.
She placed you in her lap,
adopting you as her sons,
caring for you and nourishing you,
pulling you up by the neck
until you reached the height of adults,
pulling you up by the shoulders
until you were as tall as great men.
She made you her sons' companions.
Who can say how many benefits and services you've returned to my mother
in exchange for her kindness to you?
You, Boroghul, have been my companion in battle.
Though we spent the night in the rain when no fire would burn
you didn't let me go hungry for food.
Though we were so close to the enemy that we propped each other up
you didn't let me go a night without broth.
Then when we were bringing down the hated Tatar,
the people who had killed our fathers and grandfathers,
gaining the revenge we were due,
we were killing them all,
measuring them against the height of a linch-pin.
The Tatar called Khargil Shira had escaped from the battle
and wandered out on the steppe
until finally hunger and desperation brought him back to our camp.
He came to the tent of my mother, saying,
'I am a humble beggar seeking food.'
When my mother heard this she said,
'If you are a beggar then sit here,'
and she left him sitting at the back of the door
on the bench on the west side of the tent.

My youngest son Tolui entered through the door
and as he ran out of the tent
Khargil Shira grabbed the boy under his arm
and started out the door feeling in his clothes for his knife.
Altani, Boroghul's wife, was sitting on the east side of the tent.
My mother cried out,
'He'll kill the child!'
and Altani lept through the door and overtook Khargil Shira.
With one hand she seized the braids of his hair
and with her other she grabbed the knife from his hand and threw it away.
At that very moment
Jetei and Jelme were slaughtering an ox to the north of the tent.
When they heard Altani cry out they came running,
each with an ax in his hand,
their fists still red from the blood of the ox,
and they killed Kharagil Shira.
Altani, Jetei, and Jelme then argued
over who should be rewarded for saving the child.
Jetei and Jelme said,
'If we hadn't been here,
run over swiftly and killed him,
what could Altani, merely a woman, have done by herself?
He would have killed the poor child.
The reward should be ours.'
And Altani said,
'If you hadn't heard me cry out
how would you have known to come running?
If I hadn't caught up to him and seized him by the hair,
if I hadn't pulled the knife from his hand and thrown it down,
he would have killed the child by the time you arrived.'
When she finished speaking
everyone agreed that the reward for saving the child should go to Altani.
So the wife of Boroghul,
who's like the second shaft of his cart,
saved the life of my son Tolui.
Then again, when we fought the Kereyid at the Sands of Khalkhaljid,
my son Ogodei was hit in the neck vein by an arrow

and fell from his horse.
Boroghul dismounted during the battle
and spent the night beside him,
sucking the blood clean from Ogodei's wound with his mouth.
Then in the morning he placed Ogodei,
who was too weak to ride alone,
up on his horse,
and they rode double with Boroghul embracing Ogodei from behind,
still sucking and sucking the blood that blocked his wound,
till the blood turned his mouth red.
Boroghul rode him back to our camp saving Ogodei's life.
In return for my mother bringing him up
Boroghul has saved the lives of two of my sons.
When the call to battle was shouted
and its echo was heard in the air
Boroghul never stayed behind.
If he breaks the law nine times
he'll still be absolved from all punishment."

Then Chingis Khan spoke to Old Man Usun and made this decree:
"Usun, Ghunan, Koko Chos, and Degei,
these four neither hide nor conceal anything.
They'll tell me everything that they see or hear.
They'll share with me their every perception and thought.
We have a custom of awarding the title of Beki
to a man who has proven himself to be a great shaman and chief.
Such a person should be of noble descent.
Usun is a descendant of Bagaridai,
the ancestor of the Bagarin clan.
According to this custom let Old Man Usun become a Beki.
As Beki let him dress in a white robe,
ride a white gelding, and be raised up on a seat.
We'll consult him as to the meaning of the year and the month
and we'll listen to his wisdom."

Then Chingis Khan made this decree:
"Because Anda Khuyildar was the first to answer my call

and expose his life for me in battle,
I've given the grant of orphans to all his descendants."
Then Chingis Khan spoke to Narin Togoril,
son of Chaghagan Uua, and made this decree:
"Your father fought with me at Seventy Marshes,
and because of his service he was killed by Jamugha.
Now in his memory let Togoril take the grant of orphans as his reward."
Togoril answered him:
"My brothers of the Chinos clan are scattered among all the tribes.
If Chingis Khan wants to reward me
then allow me to gather together my Chinos brothers."
And Chingis Khan made a decree:
"You may gather together your Chinos brothers
and you and your descendants may rule over them."

Then Chingis Khan spoke to Sorkhan Shira, saying:
"When I was a young man
I was captured by Targhutai Kiriltugh because he envied me,
and you, Sorkhan Shira, along with your sons Chilagun and Chimbai,
said to yourselves,
'His only crime is that his Tayichigud brothers envy him.'
You had your daughter Khadagan take care of me,
hiding me and helping me to escape.
I've remembered your service to me.
That memory has been in my dreams through the black night
and in my heart through the bright day.
Now you've come to serve me from the Tayichigud.
What reward can I offer you?"
Sorkhan Shira, standing with his sons Chilagun and Chimbai, answered:
"If you must know what I want
it's the right to camp where I choose.
I'd like to be free to camp anywhere in the territory of the Merkid
in the region of the Selenge River.
Any other rewards I would leave up to Chingis Khan."
Then Chingis Khan made a decree:
"Make your camp anywhere in Merkid territory along the Selenge.
You can choose any place you wish to make your camp

and you and your descendants will be freemen,
able to serve as archers and drink holy wine.
You may all break the law nine times
and still be absolved from all punishment."
Then Chingis Khan spoke to Chilagun and Chimbai and made this decree:
"I'll keep in mind what has already been said about you
and I'll never forget what you've done for me.
When you want to speak your mind,
when you want to ask for something you desire,
there's no need to speak to someone else first.
Stand before me in person
and with your own mouths tell me what's on your minds.
Ask me for whatever you want."
Then Chingis Khan made this decree:
"Sorkhan Shira, Badai, and Kishiligh,
all of you are now freemen.
When we attack our enemies
as freemen you have the right to take your share of the spoils.
When we go out to hunt
you can take your share of the kill.
Sorkhan Shira was in the service of Todoge, the Tayichigud chief.
Badai and Kishiligh kept Yeke Cheren's horses.
I now give them the right to be archers and drink holy wine
and declare them freemen."

Then Chingis Khan spoke to Nayaga and made this decree:
"When Old Man Shirgugetu approached our camp
along with his sons Alagh and Nayaga
he brought Targhutai Kiriltugh as a captive.
They stopped at Khutukhul and Nayaga spoke up saying,
'How can we do this to our own khan?'
You couldn't watch him die so you let him go.
Then the three of you arrived at my camp and Nayaga the Skylark said:
"We had captured Targhutai Kiriltugh
but as we came toward your camp we realized that we couldn't let him die.
We let him escape and came to offer our strength to Chingis Khan.
We'd captured our own khan

and as we came toward your camp we said to ourselves,
'He'll look at us and say,
"How can I trust these people who laid hands on their khan?"'
When I heard all this I said to myself,
'This man's acted properly because he's been guided by the great principle.'
I told them they had done the right thing and said,
'As for the one whose advice you've followed
he'll be given great responsibilities.'
Now I've given Bogorchu the ten thousand soldiers of the Right Hand to command,
and I've given Mukhali Gui Ong the ten thousand soldiers of the Left Hand to command.
Let Nayaga be commander of the ten thousand soldiers of the Middle."
Then he said:
"Let the two commanders, Jebe and Subetei,
lead armies as large as they can gather together."
He assembled all the household that had not been assigned
and gave them to the shepherd Degei to rule.
And he said:
"The carpenter Guchugur still needs people to rule,
and so does Mulkhalkhu, who's served me well.
Let them both gather people from among the Jadaran clan
and advise one another as to how best to rule them."

He rewarded all those who had helped him establish the Nation
by appointing them Mingghan-u Noyan.
He divided the people into bands of one thousand households,
appointing captains of thousands,
captains of hundreds, and captains of tens to rule over them.
He divided the people into units of ten thousand
and appointed captains of ten thousand for each unit.
Then Chingis Khan made this decree:
"Before I had eighty nightguards and seventy dayguards.
Now thanks to Eternal Blue Heaven
my power has been increased by Heaven and Earth.
I've straightened out the lives of the entire Nation
and they're controlled by the reins in my hands.
From the thousands of people in the Nation
I'll select men to serve me as nightguards, archers, and dayguards

until I've filled a unit of ten thousand."
When Chingis Khan proclaimed that he would select his new guard
he issued this decree to the entire Nation:
"Let the ablest and best-looking men step forward,
the sons of captains of ten thousand,
of thousands, of hundreds, of tens,
and the sons of common soldiers,
any man who is worthy to serve in my presence.
The sons of captains of thousands
should bring ten companions and one younger brother.
The sons of captains of hundreds
should bring five companions and one younger brother.
The sons of captains of tens or common soldiers
should bring three companions and one younger brother,
along with their own horses.
When the son of a captain of thousands comes to serve me,
the ten companions he brings will be given to him to command,
along with any animals and property given to them by their fathers.
All this will be redistributed from the units they've come from.
The same will hold true for the sons of captains of hundreds,
of tens, and of common soldiers.
Their companions and their property will be redistributed.
Any person who does not obey this order will be punished.
Any person who's accepted to serve in my presence and doesn't serve properly,
I'll send such a man out of my sight and exile him to a distant land."
Because Chingis Khan had originally chosen eighty nightguards
from among the sons of the captains of thousands, of hundreds, and tens,
now he chose eight hundred nightguards.
Then he said:
"In addition to these eight hundred
fill out the guard to make it a unit of one thousand.
No one shall stop a man who wishes to volunteer for the nightguard.
Yeke Negurin will be their captain
and he will command a thousand men."
Previously he had chosen four hundred archers.
Now he said:
"Jelme's son, Yesun Tege, will be captain of the archers,

and Yesun Tege, Bugidai, Horkhudagh, and Lablakha
will each command one company taken from the various units."
In addition to the thousand dayguards he had chosen before,
commanded by Ogele Cherbi, he said:
"Select one thousand dayguards from Mukhali's people and let Bukha command them.
Select a thousand from Ilugei's people for Alchidai to command.
Both Dodai Cherbi and Dokholkhu Cherbi will command a thousand dayguards.
Chanai will command a thousand chosen from Jurchedei's people.
Akhutai will command a thousand chosen from Alchi's people.
Arkhai Khasar will command a band of a thousand chosen heroes,
and these heroes will be the dayguards on usual days.
During battles this band of heroes will surround me."
From the tens of thousands of people eight thousand dayguards were chosen,
along with two thousand nightguards and archers.
The guard was a band of ten thousand soldiers.
Then Chingis Khan made this decree:
"This band of ten thousand soldiers will serve in my presence
and become the great middle army.
Bukha, Alchidai, Dodai Cherbi, and Dokholkhu Cherbi
will be their senior commanders."
Then he established these rules for men who served in the guard:
"When a soldier enters service in the guard
he'll serve in his place for three nights
and then change places with his relief.
If a soldier breaks the rules once
he'll be corrected with three lashes.
If the same soldier breaks the rules again
he'll be corrected with seven lashes.
If that same soldier breaks the rules a third time
he'll receive thirty-seven lashes.
We'll assume that he's found his duties too difficult to perform
and he'll be exiled to some distant place.
The company commanders will see to it
that the guard hear these rules every third turn of service.
If these rules aren't repeated the commanders will be punished.
Having heard these rules
if a guard breaks them he'll be punished.

Let no commander hold himself above the members of my guard.
The soldiers who serve me are equal to any man.
If they cause offense to any man let him come to me.
If they've done something that should cost them their lives
then I will behead them.
If they've done something they should be beaten for
then I will order them to lie down and see that they're beaten.
If any man lays a hand on a member of my guard
his lashes will be paid back with lashes
and his fists will be paid back with fists.
The members of my guard are superior to the captains of thousands.
The companions of my guard are superior to the captains of hundreds and the captains of tens.
If the captains of thousands argue or fight with my guard
it's the captain of thousands who'll be punished."

Then Chingis Khan spoke to the captains of his guard
and made this decree:
"The archers, dayguards, and cooks
will each perform their appointed duties,
and then when the sun sets
they'll give their places to the nightguard,
leaving the tent to pass the night elsewhere.
When the archers leave they'll give their quivers to the nightguard,
and when the cooks leave they'll give up their utensils and bowls.
The next morning the archers, dayguards, and cooks will return
and wait at the place where the horses are kept
until I've had my morning broth.
Then they'll announce themselves to the nightguard
and return to their places,
the archers taking back their quivers,
the dayguards going back to their seats,
and the cooks taking back their utensils and bowls.
This is the procedure that will be followed.
Once the sun has set
any person found near the palace tent will be seized by the nightguard,
held through the night and questioned the next morning.
When one company changes place with another

the nightguards coming in will present their passes and take their place,
and the nightguards being relieved will present their passes and leave.
The nightguards who lie around the outside of the tent and guard the door
will cut in two any person who tries to enter the tent at night.
If someone comes with an urgent message
let them present it to the nightguard.
They can stand to the north of the tent
and announce that they have a message to present.
No one may sit above the nightguard's seat.
No one may enter the tent without the nightguard's permission.
No one may walk between the nightguard and the tent.
No one may walk between the nightguard's posts.
No one may ask how many soldiers are in the nightguard.
The nightguard will arrest any person who walks between their posts.
The nightguard will arrest any person who asks their numbers
and will confiscate the gelding the person rode that day,
along with the person's saddle and bridle,
along with the clothes the person was wearing."
And these orders were strictly followed,
so that one evening
when Eljigedei tried to walk between the nightguard and the tent
even though he was a trusted soldier
he was arrested by the nightguards.

Then Chingis Khan spoke to his original seventy nightguard
and made this decree:
"My senior nightguard,
on cloudy nights
you lay around this tent of mine with its smoke hole
and allowed me to sleep in quiet and peace.
I've gained my throne because of you.
My happy nightguard,
on starry nights
you lay around my palace tent
and within its walls I had nothing to fear.
I've reached my high throne because of you.
My true-hearted nightguard,

in the howling snowstorms
you stood in the shivering cold,
in the pouring rain with no rest,
laying around this lattice framed tent
and knowing you're there my heart's been at peace.
The joy of sitting in this throne I owe to you,
my trusted nightguards.
When I was surrounded by my enemies
you protected me like the felt band protecting my tent from the winds.
Without blinking an eye
you stood your ground against any enemy.
My swift-footed nightguard,
before the enemy's birch-bark quivers had even moved
you were ready to meet them.
Before the enemy's willow-wood quivers had even moved
my vigilant nightguard was ready to meet their attack.
From this day on you'll be known as the Senior Nightguard.
Let the original seventy dayguard led by Ogele Cherbi be known as the Senior Dayguard.
Let the brave soldiers led by Arkhai Khasar be known as the Great Heroes.
Let the archers such as Yesun Tege and Bugidai be known as the Great Archers.
The ten thousand members of my guard will be like my private servants,
chosen from the people who make up the ninety-five bands of thousands.
Let my sons who will sit on this throne after I'm gone
not forget how well these people have served me.
Never give them cause to complain
and take care of all their needs.
These ten thousand guards will be like my guardian spirits
bringing luck and happiness to my house."

Once again Chingis Khan spoke, saying:
"The nightguard will supervise my servants,
the sons and daughters of my Palace Tent.
They'll watch after those who tend to my camels and oxen
and see that all the tent carts are in order.
The nightguard will collect all the weapons
and keep them beside the standard and drums.
They'll also collect all the utensils and bowls,

supervising all that's eaten and drunk.
Let them see to it that the sides of meat are cooked properly
and that all other food is prepared well.
If I need any food or drink I'll get it from the nightguard.
The archers are forbidden from distributing any food
without permission from the nightguard.
And when they do divide the food
the nightguard is first to be served.
The nightguard can command anyone who enters or leaves the Palace Tent.
They'll be posted at the door
and two of them will be in charge of the great wine table.
Other nightguard will be responsible for putting up the Palace Tent.
When I go out with my falcons to hunt
the nightguard will go along with me.
They'll separate into two divisions
and one division will remain with the carts in the Great Camp.
If I don't go off to fight in a war
then no member of the nightguard may go to war without me.
Any commander in my army who becomes jealous of this
and tries to break this law will be punished.
If you say to yourselves,
'How can the nightguard be excused from warfare?'
the answer is that the nightguard must always protect
the golden life of Chingis Khan.
When I hunt, they hunt with me.
When the Palace Tent moves or stops to make camp,
they must oversee all the work.
Don't imagine it's an easy job to guard me constantly.
Don't think it's easy to oversee all the carts
when my Great Camping Circle is on the move or at rest.
I say to myself,
'The nightguard must work twice as hard as the rest of the army.'
That's why I can say,
'Let them not go to war unless I go to war.' "

Then finally Chingis Khan made this decree:
"Some of the nightguard will serve as judges

and hear cases under Shigi Khutukhu.
Some will gather and distribute the weapons and armor.
These nightguard will also gather the nets used for hunting on the steppe.
Others, along with the stewards,
will divide and distribute the satins.
Once the archers and dayguards have established a new camp
then the archers such as Yesun Tege and Bugidai
and the dayguards such as Alchidai, Ogele, and Akhutai
will make their camp to the right of my Palace Tent.
The dayguards Bukha, Dodai Cherbi, Dokholkhu Cherbi, and Chanai
will make their camps to the left side.
The brave soldiers led by Arkhai Khasar will camp in front.
The nightguard who command the Palace Tent
will camp around it on the left."
Then he appointed Dodai Cherbi commander of the dayguard, saying:
"Dodai Cherbi is commander of all the dayguard.
He is responsible for all the sons and daughters of the Palace Tent,
all those who tend the horses, sheep, camels, and oxen.
Dodai Cherbi will be the constant guard behind the Palace Tent.
His food will be the remnants of grass we leave,
his fuel the dried dung that's left behind."

Prince Khubilai was sent off to war against the Kharlugh people.
Arslan Khan, who ruled over the Kharlugh, surrendered to him,
and Khubilai brought him back to Chingis Khan.
Because Arslan Khan didn't fight against us
Chingis Khan rewarded him, saying:
"I'll give him one of my daughters to marry."
Subetei the Brave, equipped with iron carts,
was sent off to war against Khudu and Chilagun,
the sons of Toghtoga Beki the Merkid.
He overtook them by the banks of the Chui River,
destroying their forces, and returned.
Jebe was sent off in pursuit of the Naiman, Guchulug Khan.
He overtook Guchulug at the Yellow Cliffs,
destroyed his forces, and returned.

Then the ruler of the Uighur people sent ambassadors to Chingis Khan.
The two ambassadors, Adkiragh and Darbai, came with this message:
"Just as we see our Mother Sun when the clouds burn away from the sky,
just as we see the flowing waters when the ice melts away from the rivers,
in the same way I rejoice when I hear
of the power and accomplishments of Chingis Khan.
If Chingis Khan will honor me with a simple gift,
a small ring from his golden belt,
a shred of cloth from his red coat,
I'll be like a fifth son to him and give him all my strength."
When Chingis heard this message he was very pleased
and he sent this reply:
"Tell the ruler of the Uighur that I'll grant his wish
and I'll also give him one of my daughters.
Let him become my fifth son.
He may come to me and take back all the silver and gold,
all the big pearls and little pearls,
all the brocade, damasks, and silks that he wants."
The ruler of the Uighur came to Chingis Khan,
taking silver and gold,
big pearls and little pearls,
brocade, damasks, and silks,
and Chingis Khan gave him one of his daughters
known as Al Altan, the golden one.

In the Year of the Hare
Chingis Khan sent off the army of the Right Hand
to conquer the People of the Forest.
His son Jochi was placed in command,
with Bukha to guide and advise him.
Khudukha Beki, who led the ten thousand Oyirad, surrendered to Jochi.
He gave himself up,
and then led Jochi back to Shighshid
where the Oyirad people surrendered to us.
In the same way Jochi conquered the other People of the Forest,
the Buriat, Barghun, Ursud, Khabkhanas, Khanghli, and Tubas.

When he arrived at the land of the ten thousand Kirghiz
their chiefs, Yedi Inal, Al Diger, and Ore Beg Digin, all surrendered to Jochi.
They presented him with white falcons, white geldings, and black sables.
From Sibir, Kashtimi, Bayid, and Tukhas,
from Teleng, Toles, Tas, and Bashghir,
the People of the Forest came to surrender to Jochi.
He took the commanders of the Kirghiz and Oyirad chiefs
and brought them back to Chingis Khan's camp,
where they presented Chingis Khan with white falcons, white geldings, and black sables.
When Khudukha Beki presented himself to Chingis Khan, Chingis said:
"He's surrendered himself and his ten thousand Oyirad
and he should be rewarded."
Chingis gave his daughter Checheyigen to Khudukha's son Inalchi.
He also gave Jochi's daughter Holuikhan to Inalchi's elder brother Torolchi.
Then Chingis rewarded Jochi for what he'd accomplished, saying:
"You are the eldest of my sons.
You've gone out from my tent to find your own manhood
and luck has been with you.
You've managed to conquer the People of the Forest
without causing suffering or bloodshed in the lands that you've taken.
All these people you've conquered now belong to you."

Later it was learned that the Khori Tumad people had rebelled
and Prince Boroghul was sent off to war against them.
Daidukul Sokhor, their chief, had died
and the Tumad were being ruled by his widow Botokhui Targhun.
Boroghul entered the forest where the Tumad lived,
riding with three of his men ahead of the main army.
As they rode through the narrow forest paths at twilight
they were attacked from behind by the Tumad sentries.
The Tumad soldiers captured and killed Boroghul.
When Chingis Khan heard that Boroghul had been killed
he immediately wanted to avenge his adopted brother's death
by leading the army himself,
but Bogorchu and Mukhali convinced him that this was unwise.
So he appointed Dorbei the Fierce to lead the army, saying:

"See to it this army follows the most rigid discipline.
Pray to Eternal Blue Heaven for success
and conquer the Khori Tumad people."
Dorbei set the army in order
and sent out spies to spread false reports,
lies about the routes they were taking and their plan of attack.
He had each man in the army carry ten rods on his back
to be used to beat any soldier who refused to keep going.
Then he equipped his men with axes, chisels, saws,
and all manner of weapons.
Rather than enter the forest by the usual paths
they cut and hacked their own road,
chopping and felling the trees that blocked their way.
Following this strategy they moved through the forest undetected
and arrived in the mountains where the Tumad lived.
Like someone leaping down through the smoke-hole of a tent,
they took the Tumad completely by surprise during a feast,
and conquered them without a fight.
Both Khorchi and Khudukha Beki had been captured by the Tumad
and they were there at the side of Botokhui Targhun.
The story of how Khorchi came to be a captive there is this.
Before Chingis Khan had rewarded him by saying:
"Let Khorchi take the thirty most beautiful women
from the People of the Forest for his wives."
So Khorchi travelled to the Tumad camp
thinking he would take away the best of their women,
but these people who had at first surrendered to us
rebelled and took Khorchi as a captive.
When Chingis Khan heard that the Tumad had captured Khorchi, he said:
"Khudukha knows how to deal with forest people,"
so he sent the Oyirad chief after Khorchi.
But the Tumad captured Khudukha Beki as well.
So when the Tumad people had been conquered
in order to honor the memory of Boroghul,
Chingis Khan gave Boroghul's sons one hundred Tumad households.
Khorchi took the thirty most beautiful women he could find
and the widow Botokhui Targhun was given to Khudukha Beki.

And Chingis Khan made a decree, saying:
"Now I'll divide up the people,
  giving them to my mother, my sons, and my younger brothers."
  As he divided them he said:
"The one who has suffered most to assemble the Nation is my mother.
  Jochi is my eldest son
  and Odchigin my youngest brother."
  To his mother and his brother Odchigin,
  who received their share together as is the custom,
  he gave ten thousand households.
  His mother felt this was too small a portion
  but she hid her feelings and didn't speak up.
  He gave to Jochi nine thousand households,
  to Chagadai eight thousand,
  to Ogodei and Tolui he gave five thousand each.
  His brother Khasar received four thousand households,
  Alchidai two thousand,
  and Belgutei one thousand five hundred.
  But when he came to think of his uncle Daritai, he said:
"Daritai has fought on the side of the Kereyid.
  For that he should be executed
  so that I never have to lay eyes on him again."
  Hearing this Bogorchu, Mukhali, and Shigi Khutukhu advised him together:
"That would be like drowning the fire in your own hearth,
  like destroying the tent over your own head.
  For the sake of your good father's memory
  only this one of his brothers remains.
  How can you have him killed?
  Since he didn't know what he was doing, leave him alone.
  Let your good father's youngest brother and his family live,
  let the smoke of their fires reach up to the sky."
  The clarity and wisdom of these words took the fire from his nostrils
  and Chingis Khan's anger was appeased
  by the counsel of Bogorchu, Mukhali, and Shigi Khutukhu.
  Reminded of his good father he said to them:
"All right, that will do."
  Then he appointed chiefs for the people he'd just divided:

four chiefs for his mother and Odchigin's ten thousand households,
and for Jochi and Chagadai he appointed three each.
Then he said:
"Chagadai is a difficult man.
It's his nature to see the smallest faults in everything.
Let Koko Chos stay beside him day and night
and give my son the benefit of his advice."
Then he appointed two chiefs each for Ogodei and Tolui
and one each for his brothers, Khasar and Alchidai.

Now Father Munglig of the Khongkhotad clan had seven sons.
The middle one of these sons was named Kokochu,
and had become a great shaman,
known as Teb Tengri, the Heavenly One.
All seven brothers conspired against Khasar
and together they beat him up.
Khasar went to Chingis Khan,
knelt before him, and said:
"The seven Khongkhotad brothers attacked me together and beat me."
But Chingis was angry with other matters at the time
and his patience was thin.
He answered Khasar:
"I've heard you say over and over again,
'There's no living creature stronger than I am.'
How could seven brothers have beaten you?"
This answer brought Khasar to tears.
Angered and hurt,
he left Chingis's tent and refused to come back for three days.
Teb Tengri arrived at the tent to speak with Chingis Khan.
"These are the words of Eternal Blue Heaven," he said.
"I have heard commandments from above about the Khan.
Once I heard voices say, 'Let Temujin rule the Nation.'
Then I heard voices say, 'Let Khasar rule the Nation.'
If Chingis Khan doesn't strike first at Khasar
none of my powers can predict what will happen."
Chingis Khan set out that night to arrest Khasar,
and two of the chiefs Chingis had given to Mother Hogelun

went to her and told her:
"He's gone to arrest Khasar."
When she heard these words,
even though it was the black of night,
the mother had a white camel harnessed to her black cart
and she set out travelling through the darkness.
As the sun was just rising,
just as Chingis Khan was tying back Khasar's sleeves,
taking off his hat and his belt,
questioning Khasar about his words and his motives,
Hogelun arrived at the camp.
Chingis Khan was terrified at the sight of her.
She rode into the camp furious,
leaped from her cart,
and the mother herself unbound Khasar's sleeves,
the sleeves Chingis Khan had just tied;
the mother herself returned Khasar his hat and his belt,
the hat and belt Chingis Khan had just taken.
Unable to control the anger she felt,
Hogelun sat down before Chingis,
crossing her legs beneath her,
brought out her two breasts from under her coat,
lay them on her two knees, and cried:
"Do you know these breasts?
These are the breasts you sucked from!
These are the source of your life,
and like the mother of the wolf
I ate the afterbirth,
I cut the navel cord for you both.
What could Khasar have done to deserve this?
Temujin could empty one of my breasts with his drinking,
and Alchidai and Odchigin together couldn't even empty one.
But Khasar could drink all the milk from both breasts.
He eased my pains and brought me rest.
So the wise and able Temujin
received his wisdom and ability from my breasts,
and from me Khasar got his great strength and skill with a bow.

Anyone who went to war with him,
he'd shoot them down and they'd surrender.
They'd be terrified by him,
he'd shoot them all and they'd surrender.
Now you claim 'I've killed all our enemies'
but you can't stand the sight of your own brother, Khasar."
Chingis Khan let his mother speak till her anger died down,
then he said:
"Seeing how angry our mother is, We're afraid of her.
We're ashamed of what We've done.
We'll take our leave," and he left the camp.
But without telling his mother
he took many of the people away from Khasar
and left his brother only one thousand four hundred households.
When Hogelun finally heard about this it brought on her old age.
And the man who had been appointed chief of Khasar's people
fled in fear to the West.

Some time after this
the people of nine different languages
all came to join the Great Camp of Teb Tengri.
Even people from the camp of Chingis Khan
came to offer their service to him.
When they heard about this
many of the people who'd been given to Odchigin
left his camp to join with Teb Tengri.
Odchigin sent a messenger named Sokhor
to request that his people be returned to his camp.
When Sokhor delivered this request Teb Tengri answered him:
"I see you and Odchigin have come to offer presents to me."
He beat the messenger to the ground and took away his horse,
sending him back to Odchigin on foot,
carrying his saddle on his own back.
When Odchigin saw that Teb Tengri had beaten his messenger
and sent him back on foot,
Odchigin went himself to Teb Tengri the very next day, saying:
"I sent my messenger Sokhor to you with a request

and you had him beaten and sent back on foot.
Now I've come myself to request that you return my people."
The seven Khongkhotan brothers surrounded him,
standing before him,
standing behind him,
and they said to him:
"What right did you have to send your messenger?"
Together they seized him and beat him
until out of fear Odchigin answered:
"I had no right to send you my messenger."
And the seven brothers replied to him:
"To show you are wrong you must kneel in repentance,"
making Odchigin kneel behind Teb Tengri.
Then Odchigin set out without the people he'd come for.
As the first light of dawn entered Chingis Khan's tent,
even before Chingis had risen from his bed,
Odchigin came into the tent and began wailing,
kneeling at the foot of the bed, crying:
"People of nine different languages have gone to join Teb Tengri's camp.
I sent a messenger to him there,
asking Teb Tengri to return the people belonging to me.
When I heard that he'd beaten my messenger,
forced him to return to me on foot,
carrying his own saddle on his back,
I went there myself to ask for my people.
The seven Khongkhotad brothers surrounded me,
standing before me,
standing behind me,
and forced me to say I was wrong,
forced me to kneel to Teb Tengri."
Before Chingis Khan could even utter a word,
Borte Ujin sat up in the bed,
pulling the blanket up to cover her naked breasts,
seeing Odchigin crying at the foot of their bed,
she began crying herself, saying:
"What are these Khongkhotad brothers doing?
First they'd gotten together and beaten Khasar.

Now why are they forcing Odchigin to kneel to them?
What kind of behavior is this?
They harm your younger brothers behind your back,
your brothers who are strong as cypress and pines.
Then when your own body falls like an old tree
who will rule your people,
these fields of tangled grasses?
When your body crumbles like an old pillar
who will lead your people,
these great flocks of birds?
Anyone who harms your brothers behind your back,
these brothers who are like cypress and pines,
will such people let my four little sons rule the Nation when they grow up?
What are the Khongkhotad doing?
How can you stand for this?
How can you let them insult your younger brothers?"
As she said this Borte Ujin's eyes filled with tears.
Hearing her words, Chingis Khan said to Odchigin:
"Teb Tengri comes to see me today.
Whatever you want to do to him,
whatever you think can be done,
I leave it to you to decide how to act."
Hearing this Odchigin rose up and wiped the tears from his face.
Outside the tent he assembled three strong men to wait for his signal.
Moments later Father Munglig arrived,
accompanied by his seven sons,
and each of the sons entered Chingis Khan's tent,
Teb Tengri sitting at the honored place to the right of the wine table.
Odchigin grabbed Teb Tengri's collar, saying:
"Yesterday you forced me to say I was wrong.
Today let's settle that by wrestling,"
and holding tight to his collar
he drew Teb Tengri away toward the door of the tent.
Teb Tengri, now face to face with Odchigin,
grabbed hold of his collar and began wrestling with him,
and as they fought there
Teb Tengri's hat fell to the head of the hearth.

Father Munglig grabbed up the hat
which carried on it the scent of his middle son's life,
and placed it quickly beneath his own clothes next to his heart.
Chingis Khan yelled to them:
"Go out of my tent.
Outside you can prove who is the strongman."
As Odchigin pulled Teb Tengri out of the tent
the three strong men standing ready at the threshold seized Teb Tengri.
They pulled him through the door,
they threw him to the ground,
they broke his spine in two,
and cast his body to the far end of the carts,
to the left of the tent.
When Odchigin walked back into the tent, he said:
"Teb Tengri had forced me to say I was wrong.
When I challenged him, saying,
'Let's settle this by wrestling,'
he wasn't willing to fight me.
He pretended to fall.
He lay on the ground and now won't get up.
He's no great adversary.
His limits are plain to see."
But Father Munglig realized what had happened
and with tears in his eyes he said to Chingis Khan:
"I've been your companion
from the time when the brown earth was the size of a dirt clod,
from the time when the seas and the rivers were just tiny streams."
Then the six Khongkhotan brothers began to press in on Chingis Khan,
blocking the door,
surrounding the hearth,
rolling back their sleeves,
and Chingis Khan, afraid for his safety, said to them:
"Stand back from me!
I'm going out!"
He left his tent surrounded by his archers and dayguards.
When Chingis saw what they had done to Teb Tengri,
that they'd broken his spine in two

and cast his body to the far end of the carts,
he had them bring out a gray tent
and place it over Teb Tengri, saying:
"Harness the animals.
We're leaving this place,"
and he set out on a journey.

They covered the smoke hole of the tent set over Teb Tengri.
They blocked up its doorway
and set people to guard over it.
Then at the beginning of the third night,
just as the sun faded into twilight,
Teb Tengri opened the smoke hole at the top of the tent
and came out of the hole with his body.
When they came to examine it later
it was decided that Teb Tengri had risen over the tent.
And Chingis Khan said:
"Because Teb Tengri laid hands on my younger brothers
and spread slander and lies to cause fighting among us,
Eternal Blue Heaven no longer loved him
and took his life and his body away."
Then Chingis Khan called out Father Munglig and said to him:
"Since you didn't control your sons' ambitions,
since you and your sons thought you were equal to me,
you've caused Teb Tengri's death.
If I'd recognized this before
you'd have been treated as rebels
and punished the same way as Jamugha, Altan, and Khuchar."
But having vented his anger on Father Munglig this way, he added:
"If you change at noon what you said in the morning,
if you change the next morning what you said at midday,
such a man's word won't be believed.
I've already given my word that you're my companions.
All right.
Let it stay that way,"
and he forgave Father Munglig.

Then he added:
"If you'd controlled your measureless ambition
who among your descendants would have been equal to mine?"
Because Teb Tengri had vanished this way
the pride and confidence faded from the faces of the Khongkhotan clan.

The Wars in Cathay and the West

After this in the Year of the Sheep
Chingis Khan set out to fight the people of Cathay.
First he took the city of Fu-chou
then marching through the Wild Fox Pass
he took Hsuan-te-fu.
From here he sent out an army under Jebe's command
to take the fortress at the Chu-yung Kuan.
When Jebe arrived he saw the Chu-yung Kuan was well defended,
so he said:
"I'll trick them and make them come out in the open.
I'll pretend to retreat
and when they come out I'll attack them."
So Jebe retreated and the Cathayan army cried:
"Let's go after them!"
They poured out of their fortifications
until the valleys and mountainsides were full of their soldiers.
Jebe retreated to Sondi-i-wu Ridge
and there he turned his army around to attack
as the enemy rushed towards him in waves.
The Cathayan army was beaten
and close behind Jebe's forces
Chingis Khan commanding the great Middle Army attacked as well,
forcing the Cathayan army to retreat,
killing the finest and most courageous soldiers of Cathay,
the Jurchin and Khara Khitan fighters,
slaughtering them along the sides of Chu-yung Kuan
so that their bodies lay piled up like rotting trees.
Jebe charged on through the gates of Chu-yung Kuan,
capturing all the forts in the pass,
and Chingis Khan led his army through to pitch camp at Lung-hu-tai.

He sent an army to attack the capital at Chung-tu
and sent others out to take all the cities and towns nearby.
He sent Jebe off with an army to attack the city of Tung-ching.
When Jebe arrived at the walls of the city, he attacked,
but he saw that it couldn't be taken this way.
So he hastily abandoned his encampment outside Tung-ching,
leaving a great deal behind just outside the city walls,
and retreated to a place six days march from the city.
This caused the people of Tung-ching to drop their defenses
and open their gates to loot the camp our army had left.
Then Jebe turned his army around,
and having each of his men take a spare horse,
they rode back across the six days march in one night,
surprising the enemy outside their walls
and taking the city of Tung-ching.
After he'd taken the city Jebe rejoined Chingis Khan.

When they attacked Chung-tu once again
the Golden King of Cathay's great general, Prince Fu-hsing,
advised his king:
"Destiny is with the Mongol.
Heaven and Earth are on their side.
Has the time come when you'll be forced to give them your throne?
The Mongol army is so powerful
they've killed the finest and most courageous soldiers of Cathay,
the Jurchin and Khara Khitan fighters,
and slaughtered so many our army's destroyed.
They've captured our trusted fortress at Chu-yung Kuan.
If we reform our army to attack the Mongol again
and once again they defeat us,
there'll be nothing to stop them from taking all of our cities.
And if these cities are forced to fight the Mongol army
they'll most likely turn against us and surrender to them.
I say we should offer tribute to the Khan of the Mongol for now,
and negotiate some settlement with him.
Once we've negotiated a settlement
and the Mongol army has returned to the north,
then we can consider among ourselves what more we can do.

I've heard it said,
'The Mongol men and their horses are consumed by diseases,
and find this southern land unfit for their way of life.'
Let's give one of your daughters to their Khan.
Let's give the men of their army heavy burdens
of gold, silver, satins, and other goods.
How can we know they won't agree to these terms?"
The Golden King agreed with Prince Fu-hsing's advice and he said:
"We will do all these things."
He sent a message offering tribute to Chingis Khan
and gave him one of his daughters as a wife.
The gates of Chung-tu were opened
and they set out great quantities of gold, silver, satins, and other goods,
letting the men of the Mongol army divide it themselves
depending on how many beasts each had to carry the load.
Prince Fu-hsing went to negotiate with Chingis Khan,
and Chingis agreed to talk with him,
accepting their tribute,
and ordered his men to stop fighting
and return from all the towns they had taken.
The army withdrew to the north.
Prince Fu-hsing rode with Chingis Khan
as far as the ridges of Mo-chou and Wu-chou,
then he returned to the court in Chung-tu.
And our soldiers carried off as much satins and goods
as their beasts could hold and went on their way,
securing their bundles with ropes of silk.

During that same campaign
Chingis Khan went off to fight the Tanghut.
When he arrived at their cities
the Tanghut leader, Burkhan Khan said to him:
"I'll surrender to you and be like your right hand,
giving all my strength to you."
He gave Chingis Khan one of his daughters, Chakha, as a wife,
and sent a message with her, saying:
"When we heard tales of what Chingis Khan has done

we were afraid of him.
Now that we see him before our city walls
we are afraid of his greatness and power.
This fear makes us say,
'We'll be your right hand and give all our strength to you.'
But when we say we'll give you our strength
remember we're a people whose camps don't move,
we're a people who've built city walls.
Though we'll be your allies
when you go off to fight a swift campaign or quick fight
we won't be able to rush off and fight beside you.
But if Chingis Khan will spare us
we Tanghut will give him the camels we raise,
the great herds of camels who flourish beneath our sheltering trees.
We'll give him the woolen clothing and satins we weave.
We'll give him the best of the birds we've trained for the hunt."
And Burkhan kept to this promise he'd made,
ordering so many camels to be given to Chingis Khan
that the herd was too large for any more to be driven.

So when Chingis Khan set out on this campaign
he made the Golden King of Cathay surrender and took many satins,
he made Burkhan Khan of the Tanghuts surrender and he took many camels.
After fighting this campaign in the Year of the Sheep,
making the Golden King of Cathay surrender,
making Burkhan Khan of the Tanghut surrender,
Chingis Khan returned and set up his camp on the Donkey-back Steppe.

But once again, in the Year of the Dog,
Chingis Khan set out to war against Cathay.
That year he sent Jubkhan on a mission
to make a treaty with the Southern Sung Emperor Ning-tsung,
and he and his ambassadors were refused passage by the Golden King of Cathay.
So Chingis Khan went off to war with Cathay, saying:
"After you've offered me tribute
how can you dare block these ambassadors I've sent to the Sung?"
He led an army to the Tung-kuan Pass

and sent Jebe with an army by way of Chu-yung Kuan.
When the Golden King heard that Chingis Khan was approaching by way of the pass at Tung-
        kuan
he sent three of his generals there,
Ile, Khada, and Hobogetur, instructing them:
"You must block the pass with your troops.
Take our finest detachment of archers for your front lines,
and hold Tung-kuan against the Mongol at all costs."
Quickly he sent these troops under the three generals into the pass.
So when Chingis Khan arrived at Tung-kuan
he was met by fierce Khitan soldiers crying:
"We must defend our homeland!"
blocking the pass.
Chingis Khan's army fought the three generals
and forced Ile and Khada to retreat.
Forces under Tolui attacked from the side,
forcing the detachment of archers to fall back,
making Ile and Khada call a retreat,
and slaughtering the Khitan soldiers as they went
until their bodies lay piled like rotting trees.
When the Golden King heard that his Khitan soldiers had been beaten
he fled from Chung-tu further south to Kai-feng,
and the troops he left behind were left to die of hunger
until they were reduced to eating each other's flesh.
And Chingis Khan was very pleased by how Tolui had fought
and gave him much praise and many rewards.
He moved his army down the Hsiwu River
and made camp on the Yellow Steppe beside Chung-tu.
Fighting their way through the Chu-yung Kuan,
forcing the soldiers defending the pass to retreat,
Jebe brought his army to join Chingis Khan on the steppe there.

When the Golden King had fled from Chung-tu
he appointed Khada to defend the city.
Chung-tu surrendered to the Mongol after a long siege
and Chingis Khan sent his cook, Onggur,

the commander of his dayguard, Arkhai Khasar,
and his adopted brother, Shigi Khutukhu,
to take account of the gold, silver, satins, and other goods of the city.
When he heard that these three were approaching the gates,
Khada rode out to meet them face to face.
He rode out of Chung-tu carrying a great load of satins woven with gold
and fine cloth of many patterns to meet them.
Shigi Khutukhu said to Khada:
"Before this day the city of Chung-tu and all it contained
was the property of the Golden King of Cathay.
Now Chung-tu belongs to Chingis Khan.
Why do you steal Chingis Khan's satins and cloth behind his back
and offer them to us here?
I won't take any of the goods that you carry."
Shigi Khutukhu wouldn't take anything,
but Onggur and Arkhai Khasar accepted Khada's gifts.
The three men counted up the satins and goods of Chung-tu and returned.
Chingis Khan asked all three:
"What did Khada give you?"
and Shigi Khutukhu replied:
"He brought out satins woven with gold
and fine cloth of numerous patterns.
I said to him,
'Before Chung-tu was the property of the Golden King of Cathay.
Now it's the property of Chingis Khan.
You, Khada,
why are you stealing Chingis Khan's property behind his back
and giving it away?'
I didn't take what he offered me
but both Onggur and Arkhai Khasar took the goods that he offered."
Chingis Khan reprimanded Onggur and Arkhai Khasar
and praised his adopted brother:
"Shigi Khutukhu has kept in mind the great principle,
that all we win is the property of the Khan.
From now on you'll be the eyes that I see with,
the ears that I hear with."

From his refuge in Kai-feng
the Golden King sued for peace with Chingis Khan,
sending one of his sons with a hundred companions as tribute,
saying: "Let him serve as your dayguard."
Accepting this tribute Chingis Khan said:
"I will withdraw my troops,"
and he took his army north by way of Chu-yung Kuan.
He sent the army of the Left Hand
commanded by his brother Khasar
along the shore of the Gulf of Chih-li, ordering him:
"Make your camp at the city of Ta-ning.
Take this city
and continue north to where the Jurchid people live.
If these people resist you, attack them.
If they surrender to you, pass by their cities.
Go north to the Taur River
and follow it back to the mountains.
Come back and join me at the Great Camp."
He sent three of his commanders with Khasar
and they took the city of Ta-ning,
made the Jurchid people surrender themselves,
capturing all of the cities along the way.
Then Khasar, riding back along the Taur River,
rejoined Chingis Khan at the Great Camp in Mongolia.

Once Chingis Khan heard that his hundred ambassadors led by Ukhuna
had been arrested and killed by the Moslems, he said:
"How did the Moslems break my golden reins?
I'll go to war with them to get satisfaction for this crime;
to win revenge for their killing of Ukhuna and my hundred ambassadors."
His Tatar wife, Yesui Khatun, spoke:
"The Khan will cross the high mountain passes,
cross over wide rivers,
waging a long war far from home.
Before he leaves has he thought about setting his people in order?
There is no eternity for all things born in this world.
When your body falls like an old tree

who will rule your people,
these fields of tangled grasses?
When your body crumbles like an old pillar
who will rule your people,
these great flocks of birds?
Which of your four heroic sons will you name?
What I've said everyone knows is true,
your sons, your commanders, all the common people,
even someone as low as myself.
You should decide now who it will be."
Chingis Khan replied:
"Even though she's only a woman,
what Yesui says is quite right.
My commanders, my sons, Bogorchu, Mukhali, and the others,
none of you have had the nerve to say this to me.
I've been forgetting it as if I won't follow my ancestors someday.
I've been sleeping like I won't someday be taken by death.
Jochi, you are my eldest son.
What do you say?"
But before Jochi could speak, Chagadai spoke up:
"When you tell Jochi to speak
do you offer him the succession?
How could we allow ourselves to be ruled
by this bastard son of a Merkid?"
Jochi rose up and grabbed Chagadai by the collar, saying:
"I've never been set apart from my brothers by my father the Khan.
What gives you the right to say that I'm different?
What makes you any better than I am?
Maybe your heart is harder than mine,
that's the only difference I can see.
If you can shoot an arrow farther than I can,
I'll cut off my thumb and throw it away.
If you can beat me at wrestling,
I'll lay still on the ground where I fall.
Let the word of our father the Khan decide."
The two brothers grasped each other by the collar,
Bogorchu pulling Jochi back by his arm

and Mukhali holding back Chagadai,
when Koko Chos, always standing at Chagadai's side, spoke:
"Chagadai, how can you say such things!
Of all his sons, your father had highest hopes for you.
In the time before you were born
the stars in the heavens were spinning around.
Everyone was fighting each other.
Unable to sleep in their own beds,
they constantly stole from each other.
The crust of the earth was pitching back and forth.
All the nations were at war with each other.
Unable to lie beneath their own blankets,
they attacked each other every day.
When your mother was stolen by the Merkid
she didn't want it to happen.
It happened when one nation came armed to fight with another.
She didn't run away from her home.
It happened when one nation attacked the other.
She wasn't in love with another man.
She was stolen by men who had come to kill other men.
The way you speak will harden the butter
and sour the milk of your own mother's love for you.
Weren't you born from the same warm womb as Jochi?
Didn't you and Jochi spring from a single hot womb?
If you insult the mother who gave you your life from her heart,
if you cause her love for you to freeze up,
even if you apologize to her later the damage is done.
If you speak against the mother who brought you to life from her own belly
even if you take back what you've said the damage is done.
Your father the Khan has built this whole nation.
He tied his head to his saddle
poured his own blood into great leathern buckets,
never closed his eyes nor put his ear to a pillow.
His own sleeve was his pillow and the skirt of his jacket his bed.
He quenched his thirst with his own spittle
and ate the flesh between his own teeth for his supper,
fighting on till the sweat of his forehead soaked through to the soles of his feet

and the sweat of his feet reached up to his forehead.
Your mother fought there beside him,
working together,
she placed her headdress on top of her head
and tucked in the ends of her skirt.
She fastened her headdress firm on her head
and pulled in the waist of her skirt.
She raised up her children,
giving each of you half the food that passed by her mouth.
Out of her great compassion she even blocked her own mouth
and gave all her food to you,
leaving her own stomach empty.
She pulled you up by the shoulders and said to herself,
'How can I make these children as tall as great men?'
She stretched you up by the neck, saying,
'How can I make him a man?'
She cleaned out your diapers
and lifted your feet to teach you to walk.
She brought you up to the shoulders of men,
to the flanks of the horses.
Don't you think she wants to see you all find happiness?
Our holy Khatun raised you up
with a heart as bright as the Sun,
a heart as wide as the Sea."
Then Chingis Khan spoke:
"How can you say this about Jochi?
Jochi is my eldest son, isn't he?
Don't ever say that again."
Hearing this, Chagadai smiled and said:
"I won't say anything about whether Jochi is stronger than I am,
nor answer this boast that his ability is greater than mine.
I'll only say that the meat you kill with words
can't be carried home for your dinner.
You can't clothe yourself in the skin of an animal
you only say you've killed.
Jochi and I are your two eldest sons.
Together we'll give all our strength to our father the Khan.

We'll cut down the one of us who strays from his promise.
We'll cut the feet from the one of us who falls behind.
Brother Ogodei is honest.
Let's agree on Ogodei.
If Ogodei stays at the side of our father,
if our father instructs him in how to wear the hat of the Great Khan,
that will be fine."
Hearing this Chingis Khan spoke:
"Jochi, what do you say?
Speak up!"
and Jochi said:
"Chagadai speaks for me.
The two of us will give all our strength to him.
Let's agree on Ogodei."
So Chingis Khan made a decree:
"Why say you'll stay together?
Mother Earth is broad and her rivers and waters are numerous.
Make up your camps far apart
and each of you rule your own kingdom.
I'll see to it that you are separated.
Don't forget what you've pledged today, Jochi and Chagadai.
Don't do anything that will give men cause to insult you.
Don't give men cause to laugh at your promises.
In the past Altan and Khuchar gave their word like this
and they didn't keep it.
You know what happened to them.
I'll give you each a band of people,
people who had once been the possession of Altan and Khuchar.
Seeing these people you won't forget your promises.
Now Ogodei, what do you say?
Tell me!"
Ogodei answered:
"If my father the Khan commands me to speak
what can I say to him?
Can I answer him no and decline?
I will say that I'll do the best my ability will allow.
Long after this day

170

if my descendants are so empty of bravery
that wrapped up in sweet grass an ox won't even eat them,
wrapped up in rich fat a dog won't even smell them,
they'll be as likely to miss the broadside of an elk with their bow
as strike the head of a rat.
That's all I have to say for myself."
Chingis Khan made a decree:
"Then Ogodei agrees.
Now Tolui, what do you say?
Speak up!"
And Tolui said:
"I'll stay beside my elder brother.
I'll remind him of anything he forgets
and waken his judgment whenever it sleeps.
I'll stay by his side and help him press on.
I'll lend him all my strength in long wars and quick fights."
Chingis Khan approved of all this and made a decree:
"Each of my brothers Khasar, Alchidai, Odchigin, and Belgutei
have appointed one of their sons to govern after them.
Likewise I've appointed one of my sons to rule.
If all of you respect this decree then all will go well.
And if the descendants of Ogodei are so empty of bravery
that wrapped in sweet grass an ox won't even eat them,
wrapped in rich fat a dog won't even smell them,
then some other one of my descendants will be found to succeed him."

Before setting out
Chingis Khan sent ambassadors to Burkhan Khan of the Tanghuts, saying:
"You've said to me,
'I'll be your right hand.'
Now the Moslems have broken my golden reins
and I'm setting out to war with them.
Send me your army to be my right hand."
Before Burkhan could even speak
his minister Asha Gambu sent this reply:
"If he's not strong enought to conquer the Moslems alone
then why does he call himself khan?"

He sent the ambassadors back to Chingis without any troops.
When Chingis Khan heard this he said:
"How could Asha Gambu say such things to us?
It wouldn't be difficult to go to war with the Tanghuts on our way to the West.
But it's enough now that we go to war with the Moslems.
If Heaven protects me,
if I manage to tighten my golden reins on the Moslem people and return to Mongolia,
then I'll see to the Tanghut."

In the Year of the Hare
Chingis Khan went to war with the Moslems,
riding off past the settlement of Alai.
He took the Merkid, Khulan Khatun, from his wives as companion
and left his brother Odchigin in command of the Great Camp.
The first army he sent out was commanded by Jebe,
behind them he sent another led by Subetei,
and behind them a third under Tokhuchar.
Sending off these three commanders he told them:
"Ride off to the outside of the Sultan's armies
and wait there until I arrive.
Then you'll attack them from your side when I strike from mine."
Jebe rode out past the cities ruled by Amin al-Mulk without touching them.
Subetei's forces also passed them unharmed,
but behind them Tokhuchar robbed these frontier towns
and stole many animals from their herds.
Amin al-Mulk cried:
"They're robbing my cities!"
and he took all his forces to join the Moslem Sultan, Jalal al-Din.
When Amin al-Mulk and Jalal al-Din joined together
they sent an army out to attack Chingis Khan.
In front of Chingis Khan's army were troops led by Shigi Khutukhu.
Jalal al-Din defeated Shigi Khutukhu's troops
and drove them back toward Chingis Khan's camp.
Then from behind appeared the armies of Jebe, Subetei, and Tokhuchar,
who fell on the Moslem armies,
killing many and breaking their ranks,
keeping them from reforming at the cities of Bukhara, Samarkand, or Otrar,

driving them back to the banks of the Indus,
so that they were forced to throw themselves into the waters
and many Moslems drowned in the river.
Jalal al-Din and Amin al-Mulk swam the river,
saving their lives,
while Chingis Khan led his forces along the Indus
where they made their camp on the Parwan Plain.
Later Chingis Khan sent Bala of the Jalayir clan
off to pursue Jalal al-Din across the Indus into Punjab.
He rewarded Jebe and Subetei for what they'd done, saying:
"Jebe, you had a different name when you fought us as one of the Tayichigud,
but now you've become my Jebe, my weapon.
As for you, Tokhuchar,
you willfully disobeyed me and attacked the cities on the frontier.
This caused Amin al-Mulk to join forces with Jalal al-Din against us.
For having done that I'll have your head cut off."
But after saying that he did not kill Tokhuchar.
Instead he lectured him about his disobedience
and removed him from the command of the army.

From the Parwan Plain Chingis Khan sent out his three sons,
Jochi, Chagadai, and Ogodei, saying to them:
"Cross over the Oxus River with the army of the Right Hand
and lay siege to the Khwarezm capital of Gurganj."
Then he sent out Tolui, saying to him:
"With your forces surround the cities of Merv."
Then Chingis Khan himself lay siege to the city of Otrar.
His three sons sent him a message, asking:
"Our armies are all assembled
and we have surrounded the city of Gurganj.
Whose orders are we to follow?"
And Chingis Khan told them:
"You will act according to the words of Ogodei."
So when Otrar surrendered to Chingis Khan
he rode from there to the city of Samarkand,
and from there to the city of Bukhara.
That summer he spent in the Sultan's former palace,

awaiting word from Bala,
making camp on the ridge of the Golden Hills,
and he sent a message to Tolui, saying:
"Join me here now that the season is hot
and the armies are making their camps."
Tolui had captured the cities of Merv and Sistan
and was taking the city of Herat when the messenger found him.
He moved his army to join Chingis Khan.

When Jochi, Chagadai, and Ogodei took the city of Gurganj
they divided the city's people three ways
and didn't leave a part for Chingis Khan.
When these three sons came to pitch their camp with him,
Chingis Khan yelled at the three of them,
Jochi, Chagadai, and Ogodei,
and for three days he wouldn't see them.
Then his three commanders,
Bogorchu, Mukhali, and Shigi Khutukhu, petitioned him, saying:
"We've made the Moslem Sultan bow at our feet
and taken his cities and people.
Your sons took the city of Gurganj and divided it up,
but it's all the possessions of Chingis Khan.
Just when our wealth has grown like Heaven and Earth,
when the Moslems are forced to bow at our feet,
when our armies are rich and happy,
why has the Khan grown angry?
Your sons know what they've done wrong
but now they're afraid of your anger.
If you continue this way you may break their spirits.
Let them come see you face to face."
This pacified Chingis somewhat and he allowed his three sons,
Jochi, Chagadai, and Ogodei,
to present themselves, chastising them loudly,
reciting ancient phrases and quoting old sayings to them in his anger,
yelling at them till their feet sank into the Earth where they stood,
till the sweat on their foreheads soaked thru to their feet,
and still he continued to censure them

until his three archers,
Khongkhai, Khongtaghar, and Chormakhan, petitioned him, saying:
"Why do you heap such abuse on your sons?
In warfare they're only immature falcons whose feathers are grey;
they're only learning what to do in war.
If you put too much fear in their hearts they won't know what to do.
From where the sun rises to where it sets there are enemy people.
Set us loose against them like Tibetan dogs
and we'll increase your strength by Heaven and Earth;
we'll bring you back gold, silver, and satins,
and many more people to rule.
If you ask us, 'Which people?' we say to you
'To the West there is a ruler
who calls himself the Caliphite Sultan of Baghdad.'
We'll go to war against him."
This cooled Chingis Khan's anger and he approved, saying:
"Khongkhai and Khongtaghar will stay by my side.
Chormakhan will go to war against the people of Baghdad
and the Caliphite Sultan."

Then he sent Dorbei the Fierce off against the city of Merv,
and on to conquer the people between Iraq and the Indus.
He sent Subetei the Brave off to war in the North
where he defeated eleven kingdoms and tribes,
crossing the Volga and Ural Rivers,
finally going to war with Kiev.

Once he had conquered the Moslem people
Chingis Khan appointed agents to govern in each of their cities.
From the city of Gurganj came two Khwarezm Moslems,
a father and son named Yalavech and Masgud,
who explained to Chingis Khan the customs and laws of these cities
and the customs by which they were governed.
Chingis Khan appointed the Khwarezm Masgud head of the agents
who governed the cities of the Turkestan:
Bukhara, Samarkand, Gurganj, Khotan, Kashgar, Yarkand, and Kusen Tarim.
And his father Yalavech he made governor of the city of Chung-tu in Cathay.

Since among all the Moslems Yalavech and Masgud
were the most skilled at the customs and laws for governing cities,
he appointed them the governors of Cathay,
along with our own agents.

Chingis Khan still waited to hear from Bala the Jalayir.
Bala had crossed the Indus River
pursuing Jalal al-Din and Amir al-Mulk into the land of the Hindus,
but he soon lost track of them there.
After attacking the people along the frontier
and taking many camels and he-goats from the Hindus,
he returned without taking the Sultan.
In the seventh year of the Western campaign,
in the autumn of the Year of the Cock,
Chingis Khan returned to his Great Camp,
pitching his tents in the Black Forest by the Tula River.

During that winter Chingis Khan said:
"I will go to war with the Tanghut people."
He reassembled his army for war
and in the autumn of the Year of the Dog he set out.
From among all his wives he took the Tatar, Yesui Khatun, as his companion.
Later that winter as they approached the land of the Tanghut,
Chingis Khan was hunting wild horses in the Arbukha region,
riding his horse known as Red-Earth Gray.
As some soldiers drove the wild horses out from the bush
Red-Earth Gray bolted and threw Chingis Khan to the ground.
The fall caused him a great deal of pain
and he pitched his camp there at Chogorkhad.
That night his condition grew worse
and the next morning
Yesui Khatun called the princes and commanders together.
"Talk among yourselves and decide what to do," she said.
"The Khan has spent a bad night and his flesh has grown hot."
The princes and commanders formed a council
and Tolun Cherbi spoke to them:
"The Tanghut are people who build city walls.

They're people whose camps don't move from year to year.
They won't run away from us
carrying off the walls of their cities.
They won't escape from us
leaving their buildings behind.
We should withdraw
and then when the Khan's fever cools
we can come back and go to war with them."
All the princes and commanders agreed with this plan
and they sent it to Chingis Khan in the form of a petition.
When Chingis Khan heard it, he replied:
"If we do this
the Tanghut will say that our hearts have failed us.
That's the reason they'll think we've gone back.
Let's send ambassadors to them from our camp here at Chogorkhad.
If my sickness gets worse
we can withdraw after we hear their reply."
So he sent off ambassadors
letting them carry this message:
"When you, Burkhan, spoke to me before, you said,
'We Tanghut will be your right hand.'
After you gave me this promise
I sent a request to you, saying,
'Now that a conflict has come up with the Moslem people
I am going off to war with them.'
And you, Burkhan, did not keep your promise.
You sent me no troops and instead sent me insults.
So as I left to fight with the people in the West I said,
'I will settle this matter when I return.'
I went to war with the Moslem people.
Since I am protected by Everlasting Heaven
I made them surrender to me and set them in order.
Now I come back to you, saying,
'Now I will meet Burkhan face to face
and I'll see why he sent me this message of insults.' "
When Burkhan Khan of the Tanghut heard this he answered:
"I did not speak this message of insults to you."

And Asha Gambu also sent a reply, saying:
"I spoke the message of insults.
 Now if you Mongol know nothing but fighting and say,
'Let's go to war,'
 well, my camp is at Alashai.
 All my tents are pitched there
 along with my wealth stored on the backs of my camels.
 Take yourselves to Alashai and meet me there.
 That's where I will fight you.
 If you're in need of more silver, satins, and gold
 take yourselves to our cities,
 to Ning-hsia or Liang-chou."
 When they brought these messages back to Chingis Khan
 he was enraged by what he heard.
 Though his flesh was still burning with fever he said:
"Yes, that answer is more than enough!
 How can we withdraw after he's said such things?
 Even if it means I die here
 we must answer these boasts with a fight.
 Eternal Blue Heaven, you decide who will win!"

Chingis Khan took his army to Alashai and fought Asha Gambu.
They overcame the Tanghut forces on the plains there.
Asha Gambu retreated to a fort in the mountains of Alashai
but he was captured there and his people were defeated.
All his tents and all the wealth stored on the backs of his camels were taken,
and all his soldiers were killed,
blown away like the ashes of a fire gone out.
Chingis Khan ordered this, saying:
"Let our soldiers kill every Tanghut they can lay hands on,
let them slaughter any Tanghut soldier they can get.
Kill the bold and the brave ones,
put every capable Tanghut man to death."

As the summer heat set in
Chingis Khan moved to the snows of Mount Chasutu,
and from there he sent out his soldiers to fight the Tanghut who lived in tents,

all the Tanghut who kept their wealth stored on the backs of their camels,
all the Tanghut who had run off with Asha Gambu to the mountains.
Then he offered rewards to his two commanders,
Bogorchu and Mukhali, saying:
"Let these two take as much as they can take."
Again he offered these two men more rewards, saying:
"I said to myself,
'I haven't given you a part of the people of Cathay.'
So you two divide between you the Juyin clan of the Kara Khitan.
Have their sons be your servants
and hold your falcons for you when you hunt.
Have their daughters be your servants
and sew clothing for your wives.
The Juyin people were the favorites of the Golden King of Cathay,
the one who killed the fathers and grandfathers of the Mongol.
Now let them serve my two favorites, Bogorchu and Mukhali."

Chingis Khan left his camp on Mount Chasutu
and laid siege to the city of Ying-li.
Once he had taken Ying-li
he moved on to Ling-wu
which stood only a few miles from the Tanghut capital.
As Chingis Khan was breaking down the walls of Ling-wu,
Burkhan presented himself with offerings for peace.
He brought out images of the Buddha made from gold.
Then followed bowls and vessels made of silver and gold,
nine and nine,
young boys and young maidens,
nine and nine,
fine geldings and fine camels,
nine and nine,
and every other thing in his realm,
each arranged according to its color and form,
nine and nine.
Chingis Khan ordered Burkhan to present himself outside the closed door of his tent.
Burkhan was told to wait there three days,
and on the third day Chingis Khan decided what to do.

He gave Burkhan Khan the new title Shidurghu,
One Who Has Been Made Upright,
and after allowing Burkhan Shidurghu to stand before him,
Chingis Khan said:
"See that he is executed.
Let Tolun Cherbi be the one to see that he is killed."
When Tolun Cherbi sent a report saying:
"I have laid hands on Burkhan and he is dead,"
Chingis Khan made this decree:
"When we were approaching the Tanghut land
to settle the words that Burkhan had sent to me,
when I had been injured while hunting the wild horses of Arbukha,
it was Tolun who advised that I take care of my life and my body,
saying, 'Let it heal,' when he heard of my pain.
Because of these poisonous words from our enemy
Everlasting Heaven has once again increased our strength
and caused our enemy to fall into our hands.
We have taken our vengeance.
Now let Tolun take the great palace tent Burkhan has brought,
along with the bowls and vessels of silver and gold."

Chingis Khan took everything from the Tanghut people.
He gave their ruler Burkhan the name Shidurghu
and then executed him.
He ordered that the men and women of their cities be killed,
their children and grandchildren, saying:
"As long as I can eat food and still say,
'Make everyone who lives in their cities vanish,'
kill them all and destroy their homes.
As long as I am still alive
keep up the slaughter."
This is because the Tanghut people made a promise they didn't keep.
Chingis Khan had gone to war with the Tanghut a second time.
He had destroyed them,
and coming back to Mongolia,
in the Year of the Pig,

Chingis Khan ascended to Heaven.
After he had ascended
Yesui Khatun was given most of the Tanghut people who remained.

The Reign of Ogodei Khan

In the Year of the Rat a Great Assembly was called.
All the people of the Right Wing
led by Chagadai and Jochi's son Batu came.
All the people of the Left Wing arrived,
led by Prince Odchigin and Khasar's sons, Yegu and Yesunge.
The people of the Middle Wing were led by Tolui,
and with him were all the royal daughters and their husbands.
This huge assembly met at Kodegu Aral on the Keluren River,
and according to the wishes of Chingis Khan
they raised up Ogodei as the Great Khan.
Chagadai raised up his younger brother as the Khan
and both Elder Brother Chagadai and Tolui
delivered the nightguard, the archers, and the eight thousand dayguards to Ogodei,
the same men who had guarded the golden life of their father Chingis Khan,
along with his private slaves and the ten thousand men who had served him.
They also gave him command of all the people of the Middle Wing.

Once Ogodei Khan had allowed himself to be named Khan
and accepted the ten thousand royal guard and all the people of the Middle,
he took the advice of Elder Brother Chagadai
and sent Okhotur and Mungetu to relieve Chormakhan,
who was still at war with the Caliphite Sultan of Baghdad,
a war his father Chingis Khan had left unfinished.
Subetei the Brave had already crossed the Volga and Ural rivers
into the lands of the Kanghli, Kipchakh, Russian, Magyar, and Bulghar peoples.
He had gone to war against the city of Kiev
and had run into great resistance there.
So Ogodei sent off an army to relieve him,
led by Jochi's eldest son Batu,

Chagadai's eldest son Buri,
his own eldest son Guyug,
and Tolui's eldest son Mongke.
Ogodei Khan sent them off to war, saying:
"Batu will command all these princes in warfare.
Let Guyug command all those soldiers who come from the Middle Wing.
Every nobleman who rules over people should send his eldest son off to war.
Let every other nobleman,
every captain of ten thousand,
captain of a thousand, a hundred, or ten,
send their eldest sons off to join in this war.
The same holds true for the royal daughters and their husbands,
let them send their eldest sons as well.
That the eldest sons should go to war is Elder Brother Chagadai's advice.
He came to me and said,
'I am sending my eldest son Buri to aid Subetei in his war.
If everyone sends their eldest sons our army will be immense
and anyone who sees it will be afraid to fight us.
In the far corner of the Earth where Subetei is fighting
the people are many and they'll die by their weapons rather than surrender.
It's said that their weapons are sharp.'
So in response to Elder Brother Chagadai's words
let us all send our eldest sons off to war."
And Ogodei Khan proclaimed to everyone
that an army should go to war commanded by Batu, Buri, Guyug, and Mongke.

Then Ogodei Khan sent a message to Elder Brother Chagadai, saying:
"I sit on this throne which was made for me by my father Chingis Khan.
People will begin to say,
'What has he done to give him the right to this throne?'
Our father the Khan never finished the conquest of the Golden King of Cathay.
With Elder Brother Chagadai's permission
I would like to go to war against the people of Cathay."
Elder Brother Chagadai approved of this, saying:
"What could stop you?
Leave a few good men behind in the Great Camp and set out to war.
I'll follow myself and send my soldiers to help you."

So in the Year of the Hare,
assigning the archer Oldaghar to command the great palaces,
Ogodei Khan went to war against Cathay.
He sent Jebe out at the head of the first army,
and they defeated the enemy soldiers,
killing them until they stood like piles of rotting trees.
They drove through Chu-yung Kuan
and deployed their soldiers to attack the cities and towns in the region.
Ogodei Khan made his camp on the Yellow Steppe
and while he stayed there he suffered a stroke.
He lost his ability to speak and grew very ill.
Diviners and shamans were called in to cure him, and they said:
"We've come to kill the people of Cathay
and rob their cities and towns,
and so their gods and rulers,
the land and the waters of Cathay
are all very angry with the Khan."
They read the entrails of several animals, and said:
"We should offer up captives,
return silver and gold,
give back their cattle and food,
and perhaps that will appease their anger."
But this didn't stop Ogodei's sickness
and the gods and rulers of Cathay only raged stronger against him.
The diviners read the entrails of more animals, and asked:
"Would you be satisfied if someone from the imperial family
offered his life to you in place of the life of the Khan?"
As they asked this question Ogodei opened his eyes.
He asked for some water,
and after drinking asked the diviners to tell him what had happened.
The diviners told him:
"Since we've destroyed the cities of Cathay,
killing people and robbing their towns
the gods and rulers of their land and waters rage against you
and they've brought on your sickness.
When we sacrificed animals to read their entrails and said,
'We'll give you whatever you want in his place,'

they only raged against you more violently than before.
When we sacrificed more animals to read their entrails and asked,
'Would you be satisfied if someone from the imperial family
offered his life to you in place of the life of the Khan?'
your sickness grew better.
Now you must tell us what we should do."
So Ogodei asked:
"Of all the princes, who is here with me?"
Prince Tolui was beside him, and answered:
"Our great father Chingis Khan
chose you to succeed him, my elder brother the Khan,
when there were brothers above and below you.
He chose you the same way one chooses the finest gelding in a herd,
examining his appearance and feeling the power of his legs.
Our father pointed at his great throne
saying it was to be yours,
and he placed the burden of the thousands of people to be ruled upon your shoulders.
Then our father said to me,
'As long as you are by the side of your elder brother the Khan
remind him of anything he forgets
and waken his judgment whenever it sleeps.'
If I were to lose you now, my brother,
who would I have to remind of the things that should not be forgotten?
Whose judgment would there be to awaken?
If my elder brother the Khan were to die
the Mongol people would be like orphans
and the people of Cathay would rejoice at our sorrow.
I will offer my life in the place of my elder brother the Khan.
I am a tall and handsome man.
I've killed the fiercest fish in the sea
and split the back of the tiger.
I've conquered everything I've seen.
Diviners and shamans, chant your songs!"
As the shamans chanted their spells
Prince Tolui drank the wine they sang over
and after a moment he stopped and said:
"I'm drunk from this.

I have to stop.
Let my elder brother the Khan decide
how he'll care and provide for his younger brother's family,
my orphan sons and my widow,
until my sons reach their manhood.
I've said all I can say.
I'm drunk,"
and he staggered out of the tent.
This is the way that Prince Tolui died.

So the Golden King was defeated
and given the name Hsiao-ssu, Little Slave.
His gold and silver,
satins and silks,
horses and slaves,
all his possessions were taken away.
Spies and agents were placed in his cities,
in Nan-king and Chung-tu,
and Ogodei returned with his army in peace,
making his camp at Kharakhorum, Black Rock.

Chormakhan finally made the people of Baghdad surrender.
Ogodei Khan knew that the land was good
and the cities in this region were rich,
and he made a decree, saying:
"Chormakhan will be our agent in Baghdad
and he'll make the people there send us ingots of gold,
brocade clothes and damasks,
big and small pearls,
arabian horses with long necks and high legs,
camels with one hump and with two humps,
and mules to carry cargo and to ride on."

The army Ogodei Khan had sent out to relieve Subetei the Brave,
led by Batu, Buri, Guyug, and Mongke,
made the Khanghli and Kipchakh people surrender
and defeated the Russians at Kiev.

As this war was being fought
a messenger came from Batu to Ogodei Khan, saying:
"With the might of Eternal Blue Heaven
and the good fortune of my uncle the Khan
we took the city of Kiev and defeated the Russian people.
We've made eleven kingdoms surrender to us.
We withdrew our forces and pulled in our golden reins,
keeping control of these people we'd conquered,
and said to each other, 'Let's hold a feast
and then we'll split up our forces and go separate ways.'
We set up a great tent and as we began the feast I said,
'Since I am the eldest of all these princes
I will drink the first bowls of holy wine.'
Both Buri and Guyug grew angry with me
and I gave them permission to leave the feast.
But as Buri was leaving, he said,
'Batu's rank is no higher than mine.
Why should he drink before me?
When women with beards become my equal
I'll drive my heel through them
and walk over their bodies with my feet.'
Then Guyug spoke, saying,
'Look at these women who dare to wear quivers.
You and I should beat them with sticks.'
Then Eljigidei's son, Harghasun added,
'We should tie wooden tails to their backs.'
I was sent off to conquer rebellious people in a distant land,
and I ask myself,
'Can we have victory when we act this way?'
Now Buri and Guyug have gone their own ways
and there's no agreement among us.
Let my uncle the Khan decide what we should do."
When the Khan heard Batu's message he grew very angry
and he wouldn't even allow Guyug an audience.
He thought of his son and said:
"Who taught this inferior child to show such lack of respect,
to speak insulting words to an elder brother?

Let Guyug rot like an abandoned egg!
If he can't show respect for an elder brother
then let him be a spy
and we'll make him climb into cities whose walls are like mountains
until the nails wear away from his hands.
We'll make him an agent
and have him climb the hard city walls
until his fingers themselves wear away from his hands.
And you, Harghasun,
who did you think you were imitating
speaking insulting words to a member of my family?
Send me the two of them together.
I could have Harghasun's head cut off,
but if I did that people would say I'd been partial to my own son.
And if Batu asks, 'What will you do to Buri?' tell him this.
Tell him to send Buri to Elder Brother Chagadai.
Let Elder Brother Chagadai decide how to punish his own son."
From the princes and chiefs at hand
Menggei, Khongkhortai, and Janggi petitioned Ogodei, saying:
"Your father Chingis Khan once said,
'If it's a matter of the steppe,
It should be decided on the steppe.
If it's a matter of the tent,
it should be decided in the tent.'
If the Khan will hear us, you're angry with Guyug.
But it's a matter of the steppe.
Acknowledge what he's done wrong and send him back to Batu."
Ogodei Khan accepted their advice and let his anger cool.
He allowed Guyug to come before him and lectured him, saying:
"When you go to war I've heard it said
there isn't a man in your army you haven't beaten;
not a soldier whose spirit you haven't broken with your brutality.
Do you think the Russian people have surrendered to us
because they were afraid of you?
Do you think you defeated the Russians alone?
Is that why you followed your violent nature
and spoke insulting words to your own elder brother?

Our father Chingis Khan had a saying about this kind of war.
He said, 'If an army is numerous then people will fear it.
If water is deep then people will drown in it.'
You go off to war sheltered by Subetei and Bujeg,
part of a huge army which defeats the Russians and Kipchakhs,
perhaps killing one or two of them yourself,
and you act as though you alone had conquered them all.
You haven't even brought back the lower leg of a goat
and you act as though you'd gone out of my tent and become a man.
You should thank Menggei, Khongkhortai, and Janggi.
They've proven to be good companions,
restraining the anger that rose in my heart.
They've been like broad spoons that calm a boiling cauldron.
So now I say to them, 'That's enough.
It's an affair of the steppe.
Therefore you advise me that Batu should deal with it.
I agree.
Let Batu set the punishment for Guyug and Harghasun.
Let Elder Brother Chagadai decide how to punish Buri.' "
And Ogodei Khan sent Guyug and Harghasun back to Batu.

Then Ogodei Khan sent a message to all of his people saying:
"Let all my subjects live in peace and happiness,
  with their feet on the ground;
  with their hands on the earth.
While I rule no member of this Nation established by Chingis Khan
will lack shelter or food.
While I sit on this throne made by my father the Khan
no one will go hungry for their daily broth.
Let every person set aside one two-year-old wether from their flocks,
and one yearling sheep for every hundred in the flock.
Let every person set these aside year after year
and give them to the poor and needy members of their units.
Then how will drink be distributed among the people,
among the imperial family with their great herds of horses,
among the commanders and guards?
Let the thousands of mares be brought in from all directions

and be milked by their herders.
After they're milked
the men who command the encampments will replace them
and become keepers of the mares,
and the milk will be distributed to everyone.
When the imperial family assembles I'll give them all gifts.
I'll fill many tents with my wealth,
satins and ingots of silver,
weapons and armor,
and grain that I've taxed from the land.
Guards will be chosen from among the various people
to watch over these tents filled with booty and grain.
When we gather together we'll divide up the lands and the waters
and I'll give them all to the people.
Isn't it right that I choose from among my thousands of people
who should rule each territory and camp?
Now only wild animals can live in the desert country.
For the sake of the people I'll appoint Chanai and Uighurtai
to be in charge of those who rule the camps.
They'll see that wells are dug in the desert
and that these wells are covered with brick.
Now I send messengers at great speed in every direction
to carry my words to all of the people.
But when these messengers must run on foot they are slow
and the entire system is a great burden to the nation.
I've thought about this problem
and decided once and for all
that a network of post stations and post horses should be established.
No one should use this network to carry messages to the people
unless the message they carry is an urgent one.
Chanai and Bolkhadar recommended this solution to me
and when I asked myself,
'Does this sound right?'
I said to myself,
'Let Elder Brother Chagadai decide.
If he approves of what I say in this message
then the decision to do this is his.' "

Elder Brother Chagadai sent these words back with his messenger:
"I think this is the proper solution to this very problem.
Let it be done!
I'll establish my own network of post stations
and join them to yours.
I'll send messengers from here to where Batu rules as well.
Let Batu also establish a network of post stations
and join them to mine."
Then Elder Brother Chagadai sent another messenger, saying:
"Of all the decrees that you've made
this decision to establish the post stations
according to Chanai and Bolkhadar's plan is the finest."

So Ogodei Khan spoke, saying:
"The princes of the Right Wing
led by Elder Brother Chagadai and Batu,
the princes of the Left Wing
led by Prince Odchigin and Yegu,
the princes, the royal daughters, and their husbands of the Middle,
the captains of ten thousand, of hundreds, and of tens
have all approved of my decrees.
What is it to them to set aside one two-year-old wether each year
for the broth of the Khan of all within the Ocean Seas?
It's good to set aside one yearling sheep from every hundred in the flock
and give it to the poor and the needy.
And it's in the interest of peace for all people
that we establish this network of post stations,
appointing captains of each station and supplying them with horses."
The Khan consulted with Elder Brother Chagadai and received his approval,
so that everyone approved his decrees.
Everyone set aside for broth each year one two-year-old wether
and one yearling sheep for each hundred in their flock.
The mares were gathered together and their herders milked them.
Men were appointed to be in charge of the mares,
the tents filled with booty, and the tents filled with grain.
Others were appointed to be in charge of the post stations and post horses.
The land was measured so that there wasn't too great a distance between each station,

and Arasen and Tokhuchar were appointed to be in charge of them.
At each post station there were to be twenty men in charge of the horses.
Then the Khan added this decree:
"Let the geldings assigned to serve as post horses,
the sheep, the milk mares, the oxen, and carts
assigned to provide for the needs of the station
all be the finest available.
If so much as a piece of rope hasn't been supplied to the post station,
the man responsible for the shortage will have all his property divided
like the body of a man cut down the middle from the back of his neck,
and half of all he owns will be taken away.
If so much as the spoke of a wheel hasn't been provided,
the possessions of whoever's responsible will be divided
like the body of a man cut in half from his nose to his feet
and one half will be taken away."

Then Ogodei Khan spoke these words:
"Since my father the Khan passed away
and I came to sit on his great throne,
what have I done?
I went to war against the people of Cathay and I destroyed them.
For my second accomplishment
I established a network of post stations
so that my words are carried across the land with great speed.
Another of my accomplishments has been
to have my commanders dig wells in the desert
so that there would be pasture and water for the people there.
Lastly I placed spies and agents among all the people of the cities.
In all directions I've brought peace to the Nation and the people,
making them place their feet on the ground;
making them place their hands on the earth.
Since the time of my father the Khan
I added these four accomplishments to all that he did.
But also since my father passed away
and I came to sit on his great throne
with the burden of all the numerous people on my shoulders
I allowed myself to be conquered by wine.

This was one of my mistakes.
Another of my mistakes was to listen to a woman with no principles
and because of her
take away the daughters who belonged to my Uncle Odchigin.
Even though I'm the Khan,   ,
the Lord of the Nation,
I have no right to go against established principle,
so this was my mistake.
Another mistake was to secretly harm Dokholkhu.
If you ask, 'Why was this wrong?'
I would say that to secretly harm Dokholkhu,
a man who had served his proper lord, my father the Khan,
performing heroic deeds in his service, was a mistake.
Now that I've done this
who'll perform heroic deeds in my service?
So now I admit that I was wrong and didn't understand.
I secretly harmed a man who had served my father the Khan,
someone who deserved my protection.
Then my last mistake was to desire too much,
to say to myself,
'I'm afraid that all the wild game born under Heaven
will run off toward the land of my brothers.'
So I ordered earthen walls to be built
to keep the wild game from running away,
but even as these walls were being built
I heard my brothers speaking badly of me.
I admit that I was wrong to do this.
Since the time of my father the Khan
I've added four accomplishments to all that he'd done
and I've done four things which I admit were wrong."

This writing is finished at the moment when the Great Assembly is convened,
in the seventh moon of the Year of the Rat,
while the palace tents are pitched at Kodegu Aral
on the banks of the Keluren,
between Shilgin Cheg and . . .

The following is a glossary identifying some of the more important characters which appear in the narrative. It is by no means intended to be comprehensive and is limited to those characters who appear on more than one occasion in the story, or whose relationship to other characters might not otherwise be clear. I have placed within brackets alternate versions of the names as they appear both in this book and in other versions of the *Secret History*. Clans are part of the Mongol tribe unless otherwise noted.

Achigh Shirun: leader of the Tubegen clan of the Kereyid tribe.

Aguchu the Brave [Aguchu Bagatur]: leader of the Tayichigud clan.

Alan the Fair [Alan Ghoa]: daughter of Khorilartai the Clever, leader of the Khori Tuman clan, and Barghujin; wife to Dorbun the Clever; mother of Belgunutei
and Bugunutei (by Dorbun), Bughu Khatagi, Bughutu Salji, and Bodonchar
the Fool, all of whom are ancestors of the various Mongol clans.

Ala Khush Digid Khuri: leader of the Onggud tribe.

Alchidai: a leader of Temujin's personal guard, selected from Ilugei's clan.

Alchidai [Alchidai Khachigun, Khachigun Elchi]: third son of Yesugei the Brave and Hogelun and Temujin's younger brother; not to be confused with the leader of
Temujin's personal guard with the same name; it is unclear why this brother
is referred to as Khachigun Elchi early in the narrative and then later as Alchidai; it is also unclear what part, if any, he played in the various battles and
power struggles.

Altan: son of Khutula Khan, first an ally of Temujin, joined the anti-Temujin alliance
along with Jamugha and Khuchar, executed by Temujin.

Altani: wife of Boroghul who saved Tolui's life.

Ambaghai Khan: grandson of Khaidu, third ruler of the Mongol clans, ancestor of the
Tayichigud clan, captured by the Tatar and executed by the Kin.

Amin al-Mulk [Khan Melig, Malik Khan]: a Muslim leader who fought alongside Jalal
al-Din.

Arkhai Khasar: warrior close to Temujin from the time of his first coronation, later a
leader of his personal guard.

Asha Gambu: a Tanghut minister who challenged Temujin.

Badai: a herdsman who warned Temujin of the Kereyid plot against him.

Bala: leader of the Jalayir clan, sent to pursue Jalal al-Din into India.

Bartan the Brave [Bartan Bagatur]: second son of Khabul Khan, father of Nekun Taisi, Yesugei the Brave, and Daritai Odchigin.

Batu: eldest son of Jochi, later the founder of the "Golden Horde" in Southern Russia.

Begter: first son of Yesugei the Brave and an unnamed second wife, Temujin's elder half-brother, killed by Temujin and Khasar.

Belgutei [Belgutei Noyan, Prince Belgutei]: second son of Yesugei the Brave and an unnamed second wife, Temujin's younger half-brother.

Bodonchar the Fool [Bodonchar Mungkhagh]: youngest son of Alan the Fair and an unknown father, ancestor of the Borjigin, Jadaran, Bagarin, and Menen Bagarin clans of the Mongol.

Bogorchu: son of Nakhu the Rich, Temujin's first retainer, one of Temujin's "four heroes" and principle commanders.

Boroghul: adopted son of Hogelun, presented to her from the Jurkin camp after their defeat, one of Temujin's "four heroes" and his personal cook, husband of Altani, saved Ogodei's life during the battle with the Kereyid, killed by the Tumad.

Borte [Borte Ujin, Khatun Borte]: daughter of Dei the Wise of the Ungirad tribe; first wife of Temujin; captured by the Merkid and temporarily married to Chilger the Athlete; mother of Jochi, Chagadai, Ogodei and Tolui.

Botokhui Targhun: widow of Daidukul Sokhor and ruler of the Khori Tumad tribe.

Bukha: a commander serving under Mukhali who led Temujin's personal guard.

Buri: eldest son of Chagadai.

Buri the Athlete [Buri Boko]: son of Khutughu, grandson of Khabul Khan, served the Jurkin subclan though by rank he should have served the Kiyad, killed in a wrestling match by Belgutei.

Burkhan Khan: ruler of the Tanghut kingdom; like the Golden King of Cathay there are actually several succeeding rulers who are referred to by this title.

Buyirugh Khan: son of Inancha Bilge Khan, leader of a division of the Naiman tribe, defeated by Temujin and Ong Khan.

Chagadai [Elder Brother Chagadai]: second son of Temujin and Borte, father of Buri.

Chaghagan Uua: leader of the Chinos (Wolf) clan, joined Temujin and was captured and executed by Jamugha after the battle of Seventy Marshes.

Chagur Beki: daughter of Ong Khan.

Chingis Khan: see Temujin.

Chilagun the Brave [Chilagun Bagatur]: son of Sorkhan Shira, one of Temujin's "four heroes."

Chilagun (Merkid): one of the sons of Toghtoga Beki and a leader of the Merkid tribe.

Chiledu [Yeke Chiledu]: a nobleman of the Merkid tribe and Hogelun's first husband.

Chilger the Athlete [Chilger Boko]: younger brother of Chiledu, temporary husband to Borte during her captivity by the Merkid.

Chimbai: son of Sorkhan Shira.

Chormakhan [Chormakhan Khorchi]: a Mongol leader in the conquest of the Khwarezm Empire.

Chotan: wife of Dei the Wise, mother of Borte.

Cyriacus Buyirugh Khan: father of Ong Khan and Jakha Gambu, former leader of the
Kereyid tribe.

Daritai [Dagaritai, Daritai Odchigin]: fourth son of Bartan the Brave, youngest brother
of Yesugei the Brave, fought both alongside his nephew Temujin against Jamugha and the Tatar, and with the Kereyid against Temujin.

Dayir Usun: leader of one of the three Merkid clans and father of Khulan Khatun.

Dei the Wise [Dei Sechen]: father of Borte, Ungirad tribe.

Dobun the Clever [Dobun Mergen]: grandson of Borjigidai and Mongoljin, brother of
Duua the Blind, husband to Alan the Fair, father to Belgunutei and Bugunutei.

Dodai Cherbi: commander of the tents following Temujin's first coronation, later a
commander of Temujin's personal guard.

Dokholkhu Cherbi: a commander of Temujin's personal guard.

Dorbei the Fierce [Dorbei Doghshin]: a Mongol commander who conquered the Khori
Tumad tribe and later fought in Iraq.

Doregene: a wife of the Merkid leader Khudu, given to Ogodei as his first wife, mother
of Guyug.

Duua the Blind [Duua Sokhor]: grandson of Borjigidai and Mongoljin, brother of Dobun the Clever.

Erke Khara: a brother of Ong Khan who sought aid from the Naiman against his elder
brother.

Ghunan: leader of the Geniges clan and advisor to Temujin.

Golden King of Cathay [Altan Khan]: actually several rulers of the Kin Dynasty in
Northern China who reigned during the late thirteenth century are referred
to by this name.

Guchlug Khan [Guchulug Khan]: son of Tayang Khan of the Naiman tribe.

Guchu: one of the four adopted sons of Hogelun, found in a Merkid camp.

Gur Khan: a brother of Cyriacus Buyirugh Khan who temporarily expelled Ong Khan
from the leadership of the Kereyid tribe; also a title given to Jamugha at his
abortive coronation and to the ruler of Black Cathay (Khara Khitai).

Gurbesu: mother of Tayang Khan of the Naiman tribe.

Guyug: son of Ogodei and Doregene, third Great Khan of the Mongol Empire.

Harghasun: son of Eljigidei who was involved in Guyug's challenge to Batu.

Hogelun [Mother Hogelun, Hogelun Eke, Hogelun Ujin]: Olkhunugud tribe, originally
married to the Merkid Chiledu, abducted and married to Yesugei the Brave,
mother of Temujin, Jochi Khasar, Alchidai Khachigun, Temuge Odchigin,
and Temulun.

Ibakha [Ibakha Beki]: daughter of Jakha Gambu, one of the wives of Temujin, later
given as a gift to Jurchedei.

Inancha Bilge Khan: leader of the Naiman tribe, father of Buyirugh Khan and Tayang Khan.

Jakha Gambu: younger brother of Ong Khan, sometimes ally of Temujin, father of Ibakha and Sorghakhtani.

Jalal al-Din [Jalalding Soltan]: son of the ruler of the Khwarezm Empire and leader of the Muslim resistance to the Mongols in the West.

Jamugha [Anda Jamugha]: leader of the Jadaran clan; anda to Temujin; then later Temujin's rival during conflicts with the Kereyid, Naiman, and other groups.

Jebe [Jirghogadai]: Tayichigud warrior who offered himself to Temujin after their defeat, a major commander of the Mongol army and one of Temujin's "four dogs."

Jelme: son of an Uriangkhai blacksmith, given to Temujin as one of his first retainers, one of Temujin's "four dogs."

Jochi: eldest son of Temujin and Borte, father of Batu.

Jochi Darmala: a member of the Borjigin clan whose horses are stolen by Taichar from the Jadaran clan.

Jochi Khasar: see Khasar.

Jurchedei [Uncle Jurchedei]: leader of the Urugud clan, faithful ally of Temujin.

Khabul Khan: grandson of Khaidu, second ruler of the Mongol clans, Borjigin clan, father of Okin Barkhagh, Bartan the Brave, Khutughtu, and Khutula Khan.

Khada: a commander of the Kin forces left to defend Chung-tu.

Khadagan Taisi: son of Ambagai Khan, fought the Tatar after his father's death.

Khadagan: daughter of Sorkhan Shira.

Khadagh the Brave [Khadagh Bagatur]: leader of the Jirgin clan and a commander in the Kereyid army.

Khagatai Darmala: leader of one of the three Merkid clans, captured by Temujin and Jamugha.

Khaidu: first ruler of the Mongol clans, Borjigin clan.

Khal: a son of Toghtoga Beki and leader of the Merkid tribe.

Khasar [Jochi Khasar]: second son of Yesugei the Brave and Hogelun, father of Yegu and Yesunge.

Khogaghchin [Old Woman Khogaghchin, Khogaghchin Emegen]: one of Hogelun's servants who tries to save Borte from the Merkid.

Khorchi: leader of the Bagarin clan, prophesied Temujin's ascension to the throne, later rewarded with the right to choose thirty wives from among the Tumad tribe.

Khori Shilemun Taisi: leader of Ong Khan's personal guard.

Khori Subechi: a Naiman soldier who killed Ong Khan.

Khubilai [Prince Khubilai, Khubilai Noyan]: one of Temujin's "four dogs" and a principal commander of his army; not to be confused with Khubilai Khan, Temujin's grandson, who does not appear in the narrative.

Khuchar [Khuchar Beki]: son of Nekun Taisi (Yesugei's elder brother), ally of Temujin, joined the anti-Temujin alliance along with Jamugha and his cousin Altan, executed by Temujin.

Khudu: son of Toghtoga Beki and leader of the Merkid tribe.

Khudukha Beki: leader of the Oyirad tribe.

Khulan Khatun: daughter of Dayir Usun of the Merkid tribe, the wife Temujin takes on his Western campaign.

Khutula: fourth son of Khabul Khan, fought the Tatar after Ambagai Khan's death.

Khuyildar [Khuyildar the Wise, Khuyildar Sechen]: leader of the Manghud clan and faithful ally of Temujin, he died of wounds received while fighting the Kereyid.

Kishiligh: a herdsman who warned Temujin about the Kereyid plot against him.

Kogsegu Sabragh: Naiman warrior who defeated Ong Khan.

Koko Chos: an advisor to Chagadai.

Kokochu (Kereyid): a servant of Senggum.

Kokochu (Khongkhotad) [Kokochu Teb Tengri]: fourth son of Father Munglig, see Teb Tengri.

Kokochu (Tayichigud): adopted son of Hogelun, found in a camp abandoned by the Tayichigud clan.

Masgud [Maskhud Khurumshi]: a Khwarezm Muslim who served as a governor under the Mongols, son of Yalavech.

Megujin [Megujin Segultu]: leader of a clan of the Tatar, defeated by Temujin and Ong Khan.

Mongke [Mongge]: eldest son of Tolui and Sorghakhtani, fourth Great Khan of the Mongol Empire.

Mukhali: grandson of Telegetu the Rich of the Jurkin clan, given to Temujin as a personal servant after the defeat of the Jurkin, one of Temujin's "four heroes" and principal commanders, given the title Gui Ong (Prince of the Realm).

Munglig [Father Munglig, Munglig Echige]: leader of the Khongkhotad clan, advisor to Temujin, father of Kokochu Teb Tengri.

Nakhu the Rich [Nakhu Bayan]: father of Bogorchu.

Nayaga [Nayaga Noyan, Nayaga Biljigur (the Lark)]: son of Shirgugetu, rewarded by Temujin for releasing Targhutai Kiriltugh, later a commander of the army who saved Khulan Khatun from harm.

Nekun Taisi: second son of Bartan the Brave, elder brother of Yesugei the Brave.

Nilkha Senggum: see Senggum.

Odchigin [Temuge Odchigin, Prince Odchigin, Odchigin Noyan]: youngest son of Yesugei the Brave and Hogelun and brother of Temujin; the word itself means "ruler of the hearth" and is commonly used as part of the name of the youngest son.

Ogele Cherbi [Ogelen Cherbi, Ogolei Cherbi]: relative of Bogorchu who joined Temujin early in his career, first chief archer and later a commander of Temujin's personal guard.

Ogodei [Ogodei Khan]: third son of Temujin and Borte, second Great Khan of the Mongol Empire, father of Guyug.

Okin Barkhagh: first son of Khabul Khan, ancestor of the Jurkin subclan of the Borjigin.

Ong Khan [Toghoril Ong Khan]: leader of the Kereyid tribe; son of Cyriacus Buyirugh Khan and father of Senggum; anda to Yesugei the Brave and adopted father of Temujin; given the title Ong by Prince Hsiang ("Ong" being the Mongol pronunciation for the chinese "wang" meaning "prince").

Onggur: Temujin's personal cook, along with Temujin's half-brother Boroghul.

Orbei: widow of Ambaghai Khan, Tayichigud clan.

Prince Fu-hsing: a Chinese/Kin general and minister.

Prince Hsiang: a Chinese/Kin general and minister.

Sacha Beki: first son of Sorkhatu Jurki, leader of the Jurkin subclan with his brother Taichu, executed by Temujin.

Senggum [Nilkha Senggum, Anda Senggum]: son of Ong Khan of the Kereyid.

Shigi Khutukhu: adopted son of Hogelun, found in a defeated Tatar camp, later chief judge under Temujin's government.

Shirgugetu [Old Man Shirgugetu, Shirgugetu Ebugen]: servant of Targhutai Kiriltugh, father of Alagh and Nayaga.

Sokhatai: widow of Ambagai Khan, Tayichigud clan.

Sorkhaghtani [Sorkhaghtani Beki]: daughter of Jakha Gambu, given as a wife to Tolui, mother of Mongke Khan, Khubilai Khan, and the Il-khan Hulegu.

Sorkhatu Jurki: first son of Okin Barkhagh, Jurkin subclan, father of Sacha Beki and Taichu.

Subetei the Brave [Subetei Bagatur, Subegedei, Subegetei]: younger relative of Jelme from the Uriangkai who joined Temujin early in his career to become a major commander of the army, one of Temujin's "four dogs," later a leader of several campaigns in Northern China, the Russian steppes, and Eastern Europe.

Taichar: younger relative of Jamugha who stole horses from Jochi Darmala (a relative of Temujin) and was killed by him.

Taichu: second son of Sorkhatu Jurki, leader of the Jurkin subclan with his brother Sacha Beki, executed by Temujin.

Targhutai Kiriltugh [Kiriltugh the Fat One]: leader of the Tayichigud clan who took Temujin captive, captured by Old Man Shirgugetu.

Tayang Khan: son of Inancha Bilge Khan, leader of a division of the Naiman tribe.

Teb Tengri: middle son of Father Munglig of the Khongkhotad clan, a powerful shaman who challenged Temujin, killed by Odchigin.

Temuge Odchigin: see Odchigin.

Temujin [Chingis Khan]: eldest son of Yesugei the Brave and Hogelun; father of Jochi, Chagadai, Ogodei, and Tolui by Hogelun; first Great Khan of the Mongol Empire.

Temulun: daughter of Yesugei the Brave and Hogelun.

Todogen Girte: leader of the Tayichigud clan.

Toghoril Khan: see Ong Khan.

Toghtoga [Toghtoga Beki]: leader of one of the three Merkid clans, father of Khudu, Khal, and Chilagun.

Tokhuchar: a Mongol commander during the Western Campaign.

Tolui [Prince Tolui]: youngest son of Temujin and Borte; father of Mongke, Khubilai, and Hulegu.

Tolun Cherbi: a Mongol commander during the second Tanghut war.

Usun [Old Man Usun, Usun Beki, Usun Ebugen]: a leader of the Bagarin clan and advisor to Temujin.

Yalavech [Yalawachi]: a Khwarezm Muslim who served as governor under the Mongols, father of Masgud.

Yegu: eldest son of Khasar.

Yesugei the Brave [Yesugei Bagatur]: third son of Bartan the Brave, husband to Hogelun, leader of the Kiyad subclan, father of Temujin, Jochi Khasar, Alchidai Khachigun, Temuge Odchigin, and Temulun, anda to Toghoril Ong Khan of the Kereyid.

Yesunge: second son of Khasar.

Yeke Cheren (Tatar): a leader of the Tatar clan, father of Yesugen and Yesui.

Yeke Cheren (Mongol): younger brother of Altan, master of Kishiligh and Badai.

Yeke Chiledu: see Chiledu.

Yesun Tege: son of Jelme, leader of Temujin's archers.

Yesugen [Yesugen Khatun]: daughter of Yeke Cheren of the Tatar, one of Temujin's wives.

Yesui [Yesui Khatun]: daughter of Yeke Cheren of the Tatar, one of Temujin's wives who accompanied him during the second Tanghut war.

Alonso, Mary E. (editor), *China's Inner Asian Frontier*, historical text by Joseph Fletcher. Cambridge, Mass: Peabody Museum, 1979.

Bawden, Charles, (translator), *Altan Tobci: Text, Translation and Critical Notes*. Wiesbaden: Otto Harrassowitz, 1955.

Boyle, John A., (translator), *The History of the World-Conqueror*, by Ala-ad-Din 'Ata-Malik Juvaini. 2 Volumes. Cambridge: Harvard University Press, 1958.

Boyle, John A., (translator), *The Successors of Genghis Khan: Translated from the Persian of Rashid al-Din*. New York: Columbia University Press, 1971.

Cleaves, Francis Woodman, (translator), *The Secret History of the Mongols*. Cambridge: Harvard University Press, 1982.

Dawson, Christopher, (editor), *The Mongol Mission: Narratives and letters of the Franciscan Missionaries in Mongolia and China in the Thirteenth and Fourteenth Centuries*, translated by a Nun of Stanbrook Abbey. London and New York: Sheed and Ward, 1955.

Grousset, Rene, *The Empire of the Steppes: A History of Central Asia*, translated by Naomi Walford. New Jersey: Rutgers University Press, 1970.

Grousset, Rene, *Conqueror of the World: The Life of Chingis-Khan*, translated by Marian McKeller and Denis Sinor. New York: Viking Press, 1966.

Hangin, John Gombojab, *Koke Sudur (The Blue Chronicle): A Study of the First Mongolian Historical Novel by Injannasi*. Wiesbaden: Otto Harrassowitz, 1973.

Heissig, Walther, *A Lost Civilization: The Mongols Rediscovered*, translated by D. J. S. Thomson. London: Thames and Hudson, 1966.

Heissig, Walther, *The Religions of Mongolia*, translated by Geoffrey Samuel. Berkeley: University of California Press, 1980.

Hung, William, "The transmission of the book known as The Secret History of the Mongols." *Harvard Journal of Asiatic Studies*, Volume 14, pp. 433–492, 1951.

Jagchid, Sechin, and Hyer, Paul, *Mongolia's Culture and Society*. Boulder, Colorado: Westview Press, 1980.

Jahn, Karl, "Kamalashri-Rashid al-Din's 'Life and Teaching of Buddha' A Source for the Buddhism of the Mongol Period." *Central Asiatic Journal*, Volume 2, pp. 81–128, 1956.

Krueger, John R., *Poetical Passages in the Erdeni-Yin Tobci, A Mongolian Chronicle of the Year 1662 by Sagang Secen*. Mouton & Co., 'S-Gravenhage, 1961.

Krueger, John R., (translator), *A History of the Eastern Mongols to 1662, Part I, by Sagang*

Secen. Occasional Paper Number Two, Bloomington: Mongolia Society, 1964.

Kwanten, Luc, *Imperial Nomads*. Philadelphia: University of Pennsylvania Press, 1979.

Martin, H. Desmond, *The Rise of Chingis Khan and His Conquest of North China*. Baltimore: Johns Hopkins University Press, 1950.

Polo, Marco, *The Travels*. translated by Ronald Latham. Penguin Books, 1958.

de Rachewiltz, Igor, *Papal Envoys to the Great Khans*. Stanford: Stanford University Press, 1971.

de Rachewiltz, Igor, "The Secret History of the Mongols." *Papers on Far Eastern History*, no. 4, pp. 115–163, 1971; no. 5, pp. 149–175, 1972; no. 10, pp. 55–82, 1974; no. 13, pp. 41–75, 1976.

Riasanovsky, V. A., *Fundamental Principles of Mongol Law*. Bloomington: Indiana University Publications, Uralic and Altaic Series, Volume 43, 1965.

Waley, Arthur, (translator), *The Travels of an Alchemist: The Journey of the Taoist Ch'ang Ch'un From China to the Hindukush at the Summons of Chingiz Khan, Recorded by His Disciple Li Chih-Ch'ang*. London: Routledge & Sons, 1931.

Waley, Arthur, *The Secret History of the Mongols and Other Pieces*. London: George Allen & Unwin, 1966.

Zamcarano, C. Z., *The Mongol Chronicles of the Seventeenth Century*. translated by Rudolf Loewenthal. Wiesbaden: Otto Harrassowitz, 1955.

TABLE 1: *The Ancestors*

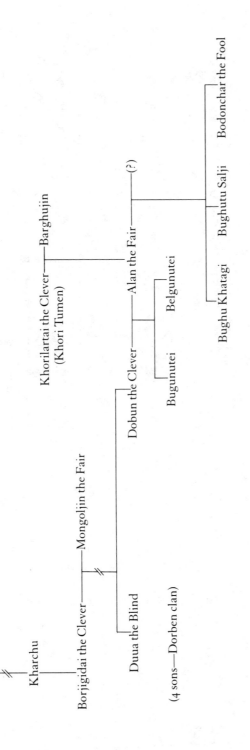

( ) = tribe or clan name throughout

TABLE 2: *Lineage of Bodonchar the Fool*

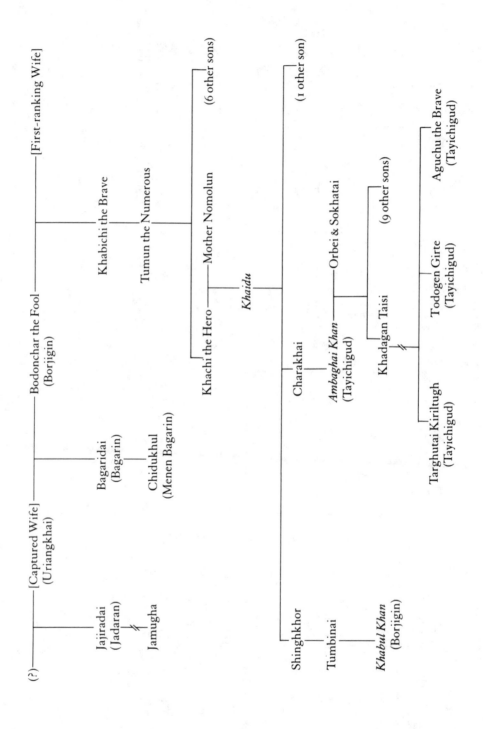

TABLE 3: *Lineage of Khabul Khan*

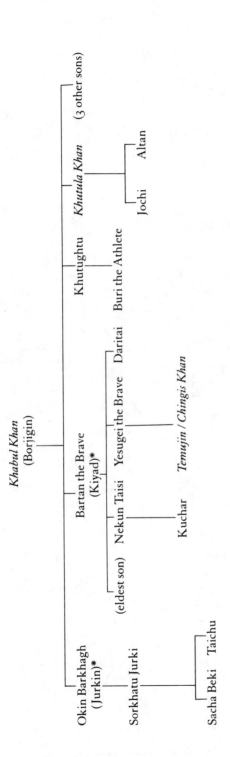

*sub-clans of the Borjigin

TABLE 4: *Lineage of Yesugei the Brave*

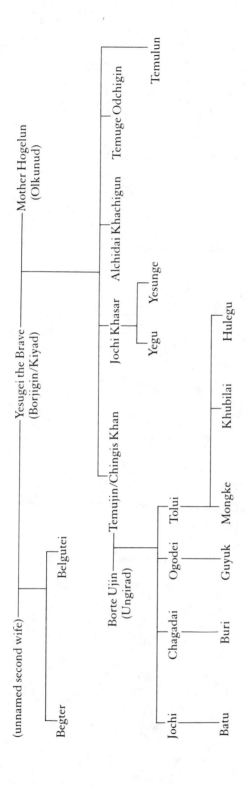

TABLE 5: *The Lineage of Chingis Khan*

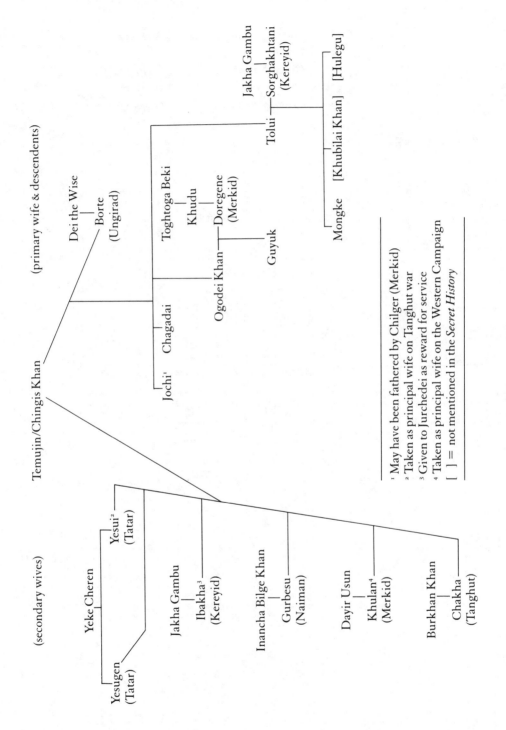

(primary wife & descendents)

Temujin/Chingis Khan

Dei the Wise
Borte
(Ungirad)

Jochi[1] Chagadai

Toghtoga Beki
Khudu
Doregene
(Merkid)

Ogodei Khan
Guyuk

Jakha Gambu
Tolui — Sorghakhtani
(Kereyid)

Mongke [Khubilai Khan] [Hulegul]

(secondary wives)

Yeke Cheren
Yesui[2]
(Tatar)
Yesugen
(Tatar)

Jakha Gambu
Ibakha[3]
(Kereyid)

Inancha Bilge Khan
Gurbesu
(Naiman)

Dayir Usun
Khulan[4]
(Merkid)

Burkhan Khan
Chakha
(Tanghut)

[1] May have been fathered by Chilger (Merkid)
[2] Taken as principal wife on Tanghut war
[3] Given to Jurchedei as reward for service
[4] Taken as principal wife on the Western Campaign
[ ] = not mentioned in the *Secret History*

TABLE 6: *Great Khans of the Mongol World Empire*

I	Temujin/Chingis Khan	(1206–1227)
II	Ogodei Khan	(1229–1241)
III	Guyuk Khan	(1246–1248)
IV	Mongke Khan	(1251–1258)
V	Khubilai Khan	(1260–1294)

TABLE 7: *Years According to the Animal Cycle*

Rat	1192	1204	1216	1228	1240
Ox	1193	1205	1217	1229	1241
Tiger	1194	1206	1218	1230	1242
Hare	1195	1207	1219	1231	1243
Dragon	1196	1208	1220	1232	1244
Snake	1197	1209	1221	1233	1245
Horse	1198	1210	1222	1234	1246
Sheep	1199	1211	1223	1235	1247
Monkey	1200	1212	1224	1236	1248
Hen	1201	1213	1225	1237	1249
Dog	1202	1214	1226	1238	1250
Pig	1203	1215	1227	1239	1251

TABLE 8: *Paragraph Numbers from the* Yuan Ch'ao Pi Shih *by Page*

The page number in this edition appears on the left; the number(s) on the right are the paragraph numbers of the Chinese edition that are the basis for the text on that page, as cited in the Cleaves translation. Text from paragraph numbers 180, 212, 215, and 278 have been intentionally omitted.

Page	Paragraphs	Page	Paragraphs	Page	Paragraphs
3	1–7	39	108–110	75	156–160
4	7–12	40	110–111	76	160–163
5	12–19	41	111–112	77	163–164
6	19–22	42	112–115	78	164–165
7	22–27	43	115	79	165–167
8	27–33	44	116–117	80	167
9	33–40	45	117–118	81	167–168
10	40–50	46	118–119	82	168–169
11	50–54	47	120–121	83	169–170
12	55–56	48	121–123	84	170
13	56–59	49	123–124	85	170–171
14	59–63	50	124–125	86	171
15	63–66	51	125–128	87	172–173
16	66–68	52	128–130	88	173–174
17	68–71	53	130–131	89	174–176
18	71–73	54	131–133	90	176–177
19	73–75	55	133–134	91	177
20	75–77	56	134–136	92	177
21	77–78	57	136–137	93	177—178
22	78–79	58	137–140	94	178–179
23	79–81	59	140–141	95	179–182
24	81–82	60	141–142	96	182–183
25	82–85	61	142–144	97	183–184
26	85–87	62	144–145	98	184–185
27	87–90	63	145	99	185–186
28	90–91	64	145–146	100	186–188
29	91–93	65	146–147	101	188
30	93–94	66	147–149	102	188–189
31	95–96	67	149	103	189–190
32	96–100	68	149	104	190
33	100–101	69	150–151	105	190–191
34	101–103	70	151–152	106	191–193
35	103–104	71	152–153	107	193
36	104–105	72	153–154	108	193–194
37	105–106	73	154–155	109	194
38	106–108	74	155–156	110	194–195